TAKE COURAGE

ENCOURAGING WORDS FOR DISCOURAGING TIMES

MATTHEW C. HARRISON

CONCORDIA PUBLISHING HOUSE · SAINT LOUIS

Concordia
Publishing House

Published by Concordia Publishing House
3558 S. Jefferson Ave., St. Louis, MO 63118-3968
1-800-325-3040 • cph.org

Copyright © 2023 Matthew C. Harrison

Many of these writings have been previously published in *The Lutheran Witness* (witness.lcms.org) and *Reporter* (reporter.lcms.org) from March 2017 to October 2022 and have been adapted for use in this book with permission.

Unless otherwise indicated, Scripture quotations are from the ESV® Bible, (The Holy Bible English Standard Version®), copyright © 2001 by Crossway, a publishing ministry of Good News Publishers. Used by permission. All rights reserved.

Quotations marked KJV are from the King James or Authorized Version of the Bible.

Scripture quotations marked NKJV™ are taken from the New King James Version®. Copyright © 1982 by Thomas Nelson, Inc. Used by permission. All rights reserved.

Quotations of John 16:33 are the author's translation from the Greek.

Quotations marked AE are from the American Edition of *Luther's Works*: volumes 1–30 © 1955–76 and volumes 56–62, 67–69, 73, 75–79, Companion Volume © 2009–22 Concordia Publishing House; volumes 31–54 © 1957–86 Augsburg Fortress.

Unless otherwise noted, quotations from the Lutheran Confessions in this publication are from *Concordia: The Lutheran Confessions*, second edition, copyright © 2006 Concordia Publishing House. All rights reserved.

Quotations identified as the Small Catechism are from *Luther's Small Catechism with Explanation*, copyright © 1986, 2017 Concordia Publishing House. All rights reserved.

Hymn texts and quotations identified as *Lutheran Service Book* (*LSB*) or its *Agenda*, copyright © 2006 Concordia Publishing House. All rights reserved.

Quotations from *Lutheran Worship*, copyright © 1982 by Concordia Publishing House. All rights reserved.

Manufactured in the United States of America

1 2 3 4 5 6 7 8 9 10   32 31 30 29 28 27 26 25 24 23

Contents

. . . .

You Have Encouraged Me

··

A few years back, my mom and dad attended church for their first Sunday as LCMS snowbirds in Florida. After the service, the pastor kindly introduced my parents and noted their relationship to the president of Synod. Later, a woman came up to my mom and said, "We pray for your son every Sunday." Just as Mom was beginning to feign humility and thank her, the woman said, "Is there some problem?" Ha! I told my mom that next time she should say, "Yes, there is a problem! He's got L-C-M-S, and it's incurable!"

I think the most humbling thing I've experienced as Synod president is the prayers of so many thousands of churches and faithful people—not only in the United States but also around the world. And I realize this has little to do with me as Matt Harrison. Rather, they all care about this wonderful gift we all share: The Lutheran Church—Missouri Synod. There have been times—some of those times very challenging—when I've actually sensed that I was being carried along in this office by the prayers of the countless faithful. Your prayers have encouraged me. They have strengthened me for this task.

Pastors often ask me, "What's it like being president of Synod?" I often respond, "It's exactly like your job, only the voters' assembly is a lot larger!"

I approach this job as I've approached every call the Lord has given me in my years of ministry—as a pastor. I am a pastor to the depth of my being. To get through the schooling to become a pastor, I worked many different jobs: processing pork by-products (messy!), detasseling seed corn, painting houses, welding, being a graduate assistant at the seminary, and others. Through all of this, I never wanted any other job than to be a pastor.

There are certain basics to being a pastor. To be sure, my calling as president of Synod is not mandated by the Bible. The pastoral office in the congregation is. It is not of the essence of the Church that we have a president or district presidents or circuit visitors. It is, however, for the well-being of the Church. Martin Luther and C. F. W. Walther repeat that over and over, and the Synod constitution is based on this truth.

Nevertheless, I perform a pastoral function very much like that of a parish pastor. I am responsible to see that the leaders, institutions, and congregations of the Synod stay true to the Bible as confessed in our Book of Concord. It's my sacred vocation to see to it that we are who we say we are. This is not easy at times. We have good (not perfect) processes that must be followed.

No pastor can make everybody happy all the time. Neither can I. Every pastor deals with a variety of situations, trying faithfully and kindly to apply the Word of God just as needed in the situation. Every pastor has to deal with rough edges in his congregation, things that need to improve according to the Bible. Every pastor has to wisely determine a course of action, often waiting for God's timing. Every pastor wants to avoid legalism or a harsh approach to delicate issues that require finesse. One of my favorite mottos is: "People follow conviction, not coercion." Every pastor has to deal with situations in which some may uncharitably judge without knowing the facts.

Sometimes I have seen the fruits of my pastoral work. Many times I have not. At times, pastoral ministry can be deeply discouraging. Sometimes you work long and hard on what you think is a perfect sermon only to have it fall completely flat. Sometimes you spend hours researching and preparing for a Bible class to have only a couple people show up. Sometimes you think things in the parish are going great only to get blindsided by complaints from an antagonist—or, worse, a friend—at a voters' meeting. Sometimes you provide Scripture and prayer in the Commendation of the Dying for a faithful shut-in as she dies, and the unchurched family chooses to have the funeral at the funeral home with a rent-a-pastor because they didn't like your funeral practices. Sometimes people get mad. Sometimes they leave. It's easy to become discouraged.

Not just pastors, but many laypeople have been deeply discouraged too, especially over the past few years. The Church is no longer culturally popular. A scriptural worldview is no longer en vogue. Jesus warned, "You will be hated by all for My name's sake" (Matthew 10:22; Mark 13:13; Luke 21:17). In most of our lifetimes, especially in our North American context, this hatred is new to us. But it's not new to many of our brothers and sisters around the world. And it's not new in the history of the Church.

Pastors stay true to the Bible and proclaim the sole, saving grace of Jesus in the context of the "whole counsel of God" (Acts 20:27). By God's grace, I intend to do that until the day I lie at the foot of an altar in a casket. Pastors know that "the freedom of the Christian" under the Gospel is one of the most beautiful teachings of the Bible ("For freedom Christ has set us free" [Galatians 5:1]). Pastors know that the Law drives us to Jesus and that the Law shows us the parameters of the Christian life. But at the end of the day, we are Gospel people, people of forgiveness. Pastors know that the church is made up of shepherd and sheep. Pastors are to lay down their lives for the sheep, as Jesus did. Pastors know that laypeople are spiritual priests, equipped to speak Christ in their contexts, to pray for all, and to serve their neighbors. Pastors know that it's impossible for the congregation to exist without the manifold gifts of leadership, business, finance, organization, mercy, and love of the people. This is the life I lead daily. The Synod at every level—congregations, districts, Synod—would quickly dissolve without our faithful laity.

Pastors are not perfect. Neither am I. That perfection was reserved for Jesus. I'm a sinner. I learned many years ago as a parish pastor that there is almost always something in a difficult situation that I can apologize for. After all, I'm not Jesus. I don't have all the answers.

So, finally, I'm a pastor. I rejoice for all the wonderful pastors, teachers, missionaries, and laypeople who are, even now, sharing Jesus in the far-flung corners of the world, at home, and abroad. The more my work has humbled me and taught me not to take stock in my own abilities and wisdom, the more I seek and want only to be bound together with my Savior, Jesus. I want to know only of His sacred wounds, His death, His resurrection for me. I want only to know His cross. He's the Great Shepherd. Worm that I am, I desire only the privilege, undeserved, to serve Him. I want only to proclaim Jesus. Only Jesus.

In all my work as a pastor—in the parish, at World Relief and Human Care, and as president of the Synod—I have been constantly encouraged by so very many of you. I know you pray for me. Know that I also pray for you. So many times I have received an encouraging note or a word of encouragement in person. In the midst of discouragement, sometimes very deep discouragement, sometimes depression, God provided you to speak His Word to me, to remind me of His promises, to encourage me away from fixation on myself and my struggles to focus on Jesus.

Now, let me encourage you. That's what I aim to do with this book. No encouragement comes from me. It's all Jesus. He is the one who commanded: "Take courage; your sins are forgiven" and "Take courage; it is I" (see Matthew 9:2; 14:27).

Jesus commands it and bids you receive courage from Him. Take courage. We're in this together, come what may.

For Such a Time as This[1]

. . . .

OUR CALLING

When Christians take up their work, they do so in a Christian way; they do it after the manner of Christ. Our daily work is our sacrifice of praise, our faithful response to the free gift of salvation. Where men answer the call to shepherd, preach, and serve at the altar, they imitate and confess Christ. But our Lord models many other works as well. Where the people of God teach, wash, and tend the sick, they imitate and confess Christ. Where the people of God listen, obey, and bear burdens, they imitate and confess Christ. Where the people of God fish, plant, and build, they imitate and confess Christ.

You know what this is: the doctrine of vocation. You know it well because it is a particular insight of Luther himself, and one that was desperately needed in his time. The people of God of the Lutheran Reformation clung to this scriptural truth. They found comfort and joy in God's assurance that their poor lives of labor pleased Him, whatever form that labor took.

THE LEGACY WE HAVE RECEIVED

When the descendants of these very people felt they could no longer remain faithful to their Lord in the land of their birth, they took this old understanding with them and brought it to the shores of

---

1 Adapted from "For Such a Time as This," *Issues Etc. Journal* (Summer 2022). Used with permission.

North America. They also traveled with an understanding of community that has been co-opted and corrupted in our time. These Lutherans knew that it takes a *Gemeinschaft* (Luther's word for "communion," "community," "church") to raise a Christian. Our forefathers brought forth on this continent a new church and understood that doing so meant erecting more than buildings with crosses on top.

As Lutherans spread across the United States following the migrations of the nineteenth century, their first priority was establishing churches led by well-trained pastors. Once congregations were secure, the next order of business was building schools. In fact, often a school building was built prior to a church building. Our fathers and mothers in the faith insisted that their children be taught by people who were formally trained in Lutheran theology. This wasn't considered normal. The only other North American Christians who had their own significant school system were the Roman Catholics.

The Lutheran insistence on building an education system in North America seemed strange to other Protestants. But after more than a century of moral and religious decay (removal of prayer from government schools, the teaching of evolution, pushing homosexual and transgender propaganda), our Lutheran forefathers have been proved right many times over. Likewise, fraternal organizations were popular around the turn of the twentieth century. They came with a variety of goals and practices, not all of which were acceptable for Christians. Rather than trying to figure out which might be okay to join, Lutherans started their own.

Another problem the old Lutherans had was that in the United States anybody could say anything. It's a great reason to move here, but it can make it hard to know which books to believe or who shouldn't be preaching on the radio in your living room. Lutheran publishing and broadcasting means trustworthy reading and listening, a way to keep learning, and a check on false teaching and secular ideas that could make their way into the Lutheran home.

Our fathers and mothers in the faith built all of this with that famous German planning and engineering: countless day schools and preschools, seminaries, colleges and universities, a publishing house, a broadcast (and now podcast) powerhouse, etc. This is our inheritance; this is the infrastructure of ministry and outreach *for such a time as this*. The six thousand congregations of our Synod have freely agreed to walk together for the purpose of helping one another. We share resources and strengths, connecting people with all that they need for this body and life, and maximizing the health and work of the Body of Christ. And it's more than the churches, schools, colleges, seminaries, books, and podcasts; it's also the teachers who know their Bible and catechism, the accountants who can tell you how to do your weird church worker taxes or make the most of your bequests to the church, the lawyers who understand the legal rights of Christians, the well-trained pastors who can actually answer your questions. We have all this because our forefathers in the faith thought we would need it and worked hard to put it in place for us.

What Is a Synod?

But what exactly have they given us? What have we received? Let's start by stating clearly what this work of their hands, the Synod, is not.

Our mothers and fathers did not build us a ship in a bottle. The Synod is not a beautiful, intricate keepsake for us to put on a shelf, never to be touched, so that we can all admire someone else's legacy and accomplishments.

They did not build us a dollhouse so we could play at being mommies and daddies with babies. *They did not build us a model train* so we could have fun pretending to be engineers and then go upstairs for a lunch someone else bought and made. Our fathers and mothers did not intend for us to have a playland that was safer and easier at the expense of being unreal.

They did not build us a monastery. Our parents' concern with passing on the faith did not include checking out of public life. They understood that Christians have a duty to society that cannot be fulfilled in isolation from our neighbors. Besides, Lutherans can't afford to spend all their time praying. Some people have to work. If you'll look back up to the first paragraph, you'll be reminded to rejoice in this gift.

My brothers, my sisters: *our parents did not build us a ghetto.* They loved us too much to raise walls around us that would eventually become our prison. Thank the Lord for this, as the world takes an ever greater interest in silencing the voice of truth and cutting off those who blaspheme its gods of pride, lust, greed, and revenge.

In the past few years, many thinking Christians have found inspiration and hope in Rod Dreher's book *The Benedict Option.* Our forefathers beat him to the punch while avoiding the pitfalls of ghetto and monastery. What exactly did our fathers and mothers give us?

They gave us an oasis where the people of God can refuel and rest so that they can return strong and refreshed to the lifelong work of evangelism and discipleship.

They gave us a consulate to help us navigate the world in which we live as aliens. The Synod is a place where people who share a language can guide one another. There are Lutherans who understand things such as money, the law, medicine, trades, travel, education, government, and other aspects of life that can be hard to figure out. It is valuable when the person helping you through whatever it is you don't know is a person who believes what you believe.

They gave us a team. Remember when your school played Zion? Never beat 'em once. And don't even get me started on the guys from Blessed Savior! Then you go to public high school, and you hardly know anybody, but there are some kids from Zion in biology. Suddenly you're pretty glad to see them. When the only face you recognize in your Spanish class is from Blessed Savior, at least you've got someone to ask to be your conversation partner, and he's just as relieved as you. Finally, a huge win: there are three people from your team in the same lunch. You might survive this (1 Kings 19:18).

Our fathers and mothers gave us a Synod. It's not a thing you experience in other places, which might be why we have a hard time understanding it. Our Savior has brought each of us to Himself. What He told His apostles is true of all of us: "You did not choose Me; I chose you." In bringing us to Himself, Christ has made us part of His Body, the Church. The energy of that Church is in its local congregations where His Word is proclaimed and His people are forgiven, baptized, absolved, and communed. So far as the Synod is congregations in communion with one another, it is church: The Lutheran Church—Missouri Synod. A Synod is also a bunch of church people who have agreed to connect themselves to one another because they are connected to Christ. No one in Synod has to be here. It is volunteer. There's no force or compulsion. That means, diagnostically, that our disagreements about things not governed by the Word of God mean less to us than the benefits of remaining together. Among these benefits are, plain and simple, the people themselves. We have formally decided to hold on to the people who love the One whom we love, for the sake of the love of Him who gave His life for us sinners.

FOR SUCH A TIME AS THIS

I don't have to tell you that our culture grows more and more hostile to the Christian faith. You can see and feel it all around you. Every major denomination has faced declining participation and membership—the overall percentage of Americans who identify as Christian has plummeted in a generation. There are now as many people who say they have no religion as there are Evangelical Christians (23 percent of the population each, according to CNN). We are a minority in a hostile world.

The Book of Esther is all about the Church's life in a hostile culture: The empire is against God's people, and a decree has been passed by the king for their destruction. But a faithful believer, Esther, has been raised up to the position of queen. But what can she do? She is wavering and sends a note to her uncle, Mordecai, for advice. He tells her: "For if you keep silent at this time, relief and deliverance will rise for the Jews from another place, but you and your father's house will perish. And who knows whether you have not come to the kingdom for such a time as this?" (Esther 4:14).

The world is hostile, but we will not keep silent; we will not freeze in fear. We will stand with one another. We will stand with Christ. By His grace we will stand and deliver the eternally relevant and life-changing Gospel of the free forgiveness of sins. Our forefathers have handed us a legacy *for such a time as this.*

The Synod's work is expressed and embodied in this infra-structure of ministry. And like any infrastructure, it gets repaired, rearranged, and reordered with the changing times. The times have always changed, and we are seeing them change now. This can be difficult. It is difficult to witness and difficult to know what decisions to make. There are many ways of approaching the day's own trouble. We should look to our forefathers for inspiration and guidance.

Well, what did they do?

They made proactive, courageous, and wrenching changes, such as getting on a boat and leaving the old country forever; such as saying "no" to forty professors from a faculty when the Holy Word of God was at stake.

They made hard sacrifices, working for the modest compensation of teachers who bring the Lord into classrooms where little children may come to Him instead of being turned against Him.

They refused to follow as Christians all around them became confused and unfaithful when asked, "Did God really say?"

These actions can only grow out of the conviction that Christ is the world's Redeemer. That is the core of our infrastructure. The bonds of love that grow around this are fed on the visible Word, the body and blood of Christ. The work that grows out of that love looks different in every generation as the Body of Christ moves through time and place. The time to break down and the time to build up are the same time: now. Help us to do this, dear Father in heaven!

One more thing. We are not the only people lacerated and hor-rified by a vicious world. As threatened as we feel by those who hate the Law and hate the Gospel, we have an oasis, a consulate, a team, a Synod. And we have neighbors who are thirsty, lost, alone, shut out. People are looking for help. By the grace of God, we can offer it.

What is that help? It is making sure that Light pours out of our stained-glass windows, a beacon for all who are desperate to be delivered out of darkness. It is submitting with joy to the gathering work of the Holy Spirit, who calls us to the very house of God. It is telling a friend who is waiting for a Savior, "Come and see." It is trusting that God's Word will not return void. It is laboring under that miraculous alloy of humility and fearlessness, the mettle of repentant sinners who know that their Redeemer lives.

It is knowing that what every sad, scared, anxious, angry, hungry, sick, shackled, bitter, toxic person needs is Jesus, and there aren't any tricks to making that introduction.

Friends, we have work to do. The Lord is our strength, and He has added unto us good friends, faithful neighbors, and the like. If you are not sure how to begin, I suggest that you *make the sign of the holy cross and say:*

> In the name of the Father and of the ☩ Son and of the Holy Spirit. Amen.

> Then, kneeling or standing, repeat the Creed and the Lord's Prayer.

> Then go joyfully to your work, singing a hymn, like that of the Ten Commandments, or whatever your devotion may suggest. (Small Catechism, Daily Prayers)

Why Are You So Afraid?

············

Fear is pervasive, today and yesterday. After his sin, Adam was afraid of God and hid: "I heard the sound of You in the garden, and I was afraid, because I was naked, and I hid myself" (Genesis 3:10). Sarah denied laughing because she was afraid (Genesis 18:15). Jacob was afraid of God (Genesis 28:16–17), of Laban (Genesis 31:31), and of Esau (Genesis 32:7). Joseph's brothers were afraid of him (Genesis 43:18).

Moses was afraid of God (Exodus 3:6), and so were the Israelites (Exodus 20:18). When Moses' face was shining, having been in the presence of God, the Israelites were afraid to look at his face too (Exodus 34:30). The Israelites were afraid of the Philistines (1 Samuel 7:7) and the other inhabitants of the land of Canaan. When God brought His people back from exile, they were again afraid of the inhabitants in the land (Ezra 4:4).

The story is the same throughout the New Testament.

- Zechariah was *afraid* of the angel (Luke 1:13), as was Mary (Luke 1:30).

- After Jesus orchestrated a miraculous catch of fish, Peter fell to his knees, *afraid* (Luke 5:8–10).

- When they believed their lives were in peril from a great windstorm and big waves, the disciples in the boat were *afraid*; later, after Jesus stilled the storm with a word, they were *filled with fear*, wondering who it was whom wind and sea would obey (Mark 4:37–41).

- When they saw Jesus walking on water, the disciples were *terrified* (Matthew 14:26). When Peter walked out to Jesus and "saw the wind," he was *afraid* (v. 30).

- Peter, James, and John were *terrified* at Jesus' transfiguration (Mark 9:6).

- The disciples were *afraid* to ask Jesus the meaning of His prediction of His death and resurrection (Mark 9:32).

- The Easter Gospel ends: "And they went out and fled from the tomb, for trembling and astonishment had seized them, and they said nothing to anyone, for they were *afraid*" (Mark 16:8).

Fear, especially among Jesus' disciples, was exceedingly common. Today, too, fear is all too common among Christians. All these varieties of fear are not the same, though. Some fear is meet, right, and salutary. Some fear is not.

After calming the storm that had caused His disciples to fear for their lives, Jesus turns to the real danger. "Why are you so afraid? Have you still no faith?" (Mark 4:40). The catechism rightly includes fear as a component of the faith the First Commandment calls us to have. But the fear Jesus rebukes is opposed to faith. "The fear of the LORD is the beginning of wisdom" (Proverbs 9:10), but fear of anything else is the beginning of idolatry.

After Jesus stills the storm, His disciples' fear shifts from their temporary predicament to their eternal one. "And they were filled with great fear and said to one another, 'Who then is this, that even the wind and the sea obey Him?'" (Mark 4:41).

This exhortation to courage is not a call away from fear, but a call to proper fear. Courage is not the absence of fear. Some have said that courage is fear that has said its prayers. I prefer to say that courage is fear that has been baptized.

Every Crisis Is Temporary

There really is "nothing new under the sun" (Ecclesiastes 1:9). Pandemics and plagues have come and gone throughout the millennia. Christ has sustained His Church. When the bacteria-borne Black Plague struck Wittenberg in Luther's day, he wrote a letter of counsel to a good friend:

> Use medicine; take potions which can help you; fumigate house, yard, and street; shun persons and places wherever your neighbor does not need your presence or has recovered, and act like a man who wants to help put out the burning city. What else is the epidemic but a fire which instead of consuming wood and straw devours life and body? You ought to think this way: "Very well, by God's decree the enemy has sent us poison and deadly offal. Therefore, I shall ask God mercifully to protect us." Then I shall fumigate, help purify the air, administer medicine, and take it. I shall avoid places and persons where my presence is not needed in order not to become contaminated and thus perchance infect and pollute others, and so cause their death as a result of my negligence. If God should wish to take me, he will surely find me and I have done what he has expected of me and so I am not responsible for either my own death or the death of others. If my neighbor needs me, however, I shall not avoid place or person but will go freely. . . . See, this is such a God-fearing faith because it is neither brash nor foolhardy and does not tempt God.[1]

Luther says he would "go freely" because he decided to remain in the city and provide spiritual care even as his parishioners, dear friends, and loved ones died. Today, medical professionals place themselves in danger to serve those with contagious illnesses.

---

1   *Whether One May Flee from a Deadly Plague*, AE 43:131–32.

OUR CURRENT TROUBLES POINT US TO ETERNITY

Luther most likely wrote our favorite Reformation hymn "A Mighty Fortress Is Our God" around 1527—during the plague. Temporal tragedy points us to eternal hope and consolation. Jesus foretold what we see: "Nation will rise against nation, and kingdom against kingdom. There will be great earthquakes, and in various places famines and pestilences. And there will be terrors and great signs from heaven" (Luke 21:10–11).

We see such things now. Great fear has spread across the globe. Confusion abounds. The church is stressed and pressed. LCMS pastors have been in deep distress as parishioners died in hospital quarantine, cut off from spiritual care. Virtually all of us have had to forgo gathering as the church, receiving the Sacrament from our pastors only in small groups or not at all. Many of us have been deeply troubled by governments mandating things even within our sanctuaries! (Acts 5:29).

Jesus also reassures us: "Now when these things begin to take place, straighten up and raise your heads, because your redemption is drawing near" (Luke 21:28). We have been redeemed, paid for by Christ's death on the cross, declared righteous by His resurrection (Romans 4:25). We anxiously await the "redemption of our bodies" (Romans 8:23)—that is, the resurrection of our bodies to live with Christ for eternity. We do not cower, least of all in the face of a pandemic. "Straighten up!" says Jesus. "Lift up your heads." "Surely I am coming soon" (Revelation 22:20).

THIS CRISIS DEFINES OUR TASK TODAY

I'm worried. I'm forever self-centered. I'm a sinner. Crises move me to repentance. Thank God I'm forgiven. But not all fear is sinful. It's not sinful to run and get out of the way of a tornado or an oncoming train. We are using our God-given smarts when we wisely follow the advice of medical authorities. How shall I live now? "It is no longer

I who live, but Christ who lives in me. And the life I now live in the flesh I live by faith in the Son of God, who loved me and gave Himself for me" (Galatians 2:20).

As Luther acted during the plague, and as he once said, "The need of my neighbor is my call to mercy." What is my vocation? I shall honor government officials (Fourth Commandment)—specifically as they ask and require me to act responsibly regarding my own health and that of others (Fifth Commandment), but not where government dictates matters of the faith. Where I am called to serve others, even at some risk to myself (Luther left this decision to the individual conscience), so shall I do, trusting that God is my helper and that I'm in His hands. I shall do my best to demonstrate love to others, especially to my family and the friends God has given me. I shall be generous in my prayers for all, especially my pastors, church workers, and congregation. I shall pray for those in authority. When I cannot gather with others for worship, I shall concentrate on the Word of God. I shall continue to be generous in my stewardship and a blessing to the mission of my congregation and Synod so that others may know Christ.

CRISIS FORCES US TO ASK: "HOW SHALL WE ACT WHEN IT'S OVER?"

Crises always force us to ask foundational questions.

- Who is Christ?
- What does the church mean in our lives?
- How are we relating to our families?
- Are we living lives of fear or of joyfulness in Christ's abundant gifts?
- What have we learned about our congregation and community?
- What have we learned about reaching out?
- What renewed or new appreciation do we have for our congregation?

- What have we learned about caring for one another within the congregation?

- Is our congregation really caring for its pastors and workers?

- What have we learned about the blessing of being in this together as the LCMS?

- Have we found strength in the fundamental teachings of the catechism?

- What have we learned from the Scriptures about faith and life?

- How might we work together with nearby LCMS congregations for the sake of the Gospel?

- How might we better prepare for the next crisis?

Even as you think through some of these things, count on the fact that "for those who love God all things work together for good, for those who are called according to His purpose" (Romans 8:28). And for that reason, we can dare in Christ to be confident that we shall be stronger for passing through crisis—stronger together.

How Scripture Speaks of Courage

··

How does Jesus deal with fear? "*Take courage*," He says. The Greeks called it θάρσει (pronounced *tharsei*), and it tells us how we *should* respond to our own fear.

θάρσει (*THARSEI*)

In Matthew 9, Jesus says it twice. First, when Jesus returned to His hometown, some people carried to Him a paralyzed man on his mat. "When Jesus saw their faith, He said to the paralytic, '*Tharsei*, my son; your sins are forgiven'" (v. 2).

Second, while Jesus is following a ruler of the synagogue to his house in order to heal his daughter, a woman who had suffered for twelve years with a discharge of blood comes up to Him secretly, thinking, "If I only touch His garment, I will be made well" (v. 21). Each of the Synoptic Gospels (Matthew, Mark, and Luke) includes this story. In both Mark's and Luke's accounts, the woman is healed immediately before Jesus speaks to her. Matthew moves straight from her touch to Jesus' words to her. And what does He say? "*Tharsei*, daughter; your faith has made you well" (v. 22).

In most modern English translations, *tharsei* is translated "take heart." That's a fine translation, but to our modern ears "hearts" can sound a little Hallmark-y. *Tharsei* comes from a verb that means "to be of good courage," but in the New Testament it's only used as an imperative, a command. *Take courage!*

Θαρσεῖτε (*Tharseite*)

Twice Jesus uses the command as a plural, spoken to the group of His disciples. In Mark 6, Jesus left His disciples to go up on a mountain to pray. Meanwhile, they left in a boat to cross the Sea of Galilee. In the fourth watch of the night, or just before dawn, Jesus was walking on the water across the sea. The disciples thought He was a ghost and cried out in fear. St. Mark records that Jesus was intending to pass by His disciples, but upon hearing their cries and knowing their fear, Jesus immediately called out to them: "*Tharseite*; it is I. Do not be afraid." *Take courage! It is I!*

Trampling the waves of the sea (Job 9:8) is just one of the characteristics of God that caused Job to ask, "How can man be in the right before God?" (v. 2). He moves mountains; He shakes the earth; He commands the sun; He seals up the stars; He alone stretched out the heavens; He does marvelous things (Job 9:2–12). He who does all these marvelous things is the one who bids His disciples: "Take courage! It is I!"

The second time Jesus exhorted His disciples as a group was in John 16, at the very end of His long catechesis with them on the night before He was betrayed. He had promised His departure, His sending of the Holy Spirit, and coming persecution. The disciples were confused: "'What is this that He says to us, "A little while, and you will not see Me, and again a little while, and you will see Me"; and, "because I am going to the Father"?' So they were saying, 'What does He mean by "a little while"? We do not know what He is talking about'" (John 16:17–18).

After some more "figures of speech," Jesus explained:

I have said these things to you in figures of speech. The hour is coming when I will no longer speak to you in figures of speech but will tell you plainly about the Father. In that day you will ask in My name, and I do not say to you that I will ask the Father on your behalf; for the Father Himself loves you, because you have loved Me and have believed that I came from God. I came from the Father and

> have come into the world, and now I am leaving the world and going to the Father. (vv. 25–28)

Finally, this made sense to the men.

> "Ah, now You are speaking plainly and not using figurative speech! Now we know that You know all things and do not need anyone to question You; this is why we believe that You came from God." Jesus answered them, "Do you now believe? Behold, the hour is coming, indeed it has come, when you will be scattered, each to his own home, and will leave Me alone. Yet I am not alone, for the Father is with Me. I have said these things to you, that in Me you may have peace. In the world you will have tribulation. But *tharseite*; I have overcome the world." (vv. 29–33)

In the world you will have tribulation. That's guaranteed. The world hates the Gospel, the Good News of free and full forgiveness for sinners for the sake of the death on the cross of the incarnate God. Since Pentecost, the Church has endured constant tribulation. It waxes and wanes, varies from place to place, but the Lord's Church has never been free from tribulation and persecution. But *take courage*. Jesus has overcome the world. Not even the gates of hell can triumph against His Church (Matthew 16:18).

Scripture is replete with these exhortations to have courage for the sake of Jesus, the eternal Word of God.

- When Jesus hears blind Bartimaeus calling "Jesus, Son of David, have mercy on me!" He calls for him. The crowd tells Bartimaeus, "*Take courage!* Get up; He is calling you" (Mark 10:46–52, especially v. 49).

- After St. Paul has testified before the council, been punched in the mouth for defending himself, incited a violent altercation between Pharisees and Sadducees, and been taken by force to the soldiers' barracks, Jesus "stood by him and said, '*Take courage*, for as you have testified to the facts about Me in Jerusalem, so you must testify also in Rome'" (Acts 23:1–11, especially v. 11).

- Psalm 27 begins: "The Lord is my light and my salvation; whom shall I fear? The Lord is the stronghold of my life; of whom shall be afraid?"

  > When evildoers assail me
  > to eat up my flesh,
  > my adversaries and foes,
  > it is they who stumble and fall.
  > Though an army encamp against me,
  > my heart shall not fear;
  > though war arise against me,
  > yet I will be confident. (vv. 1–3)

  The psalmist concludes: "Wait for the Lord; be strong, and *let your heart take courage*; wait for the Lord!" (v. 14).

- Again in Psalm 31: "Be strong, and *let your heart take courage*, all you who wait for the Lord!" (v. 24).

- After Jesus died, "Joseph of Arimathea, a respected member of the council, who was also himself looking for the kingdom of God, *took courage* and went to Pilate and asked for the body of Jesus" (Mark 15:43).

- St. Paul wrote to the Philippians: "I will rejoice, for I know that through your prayers and the help of the Spirit of Jesus Christ this will turn out for my deliverance, as it is my eager expectation and hope that I will not be at all ashamed, but that *with full courage* now as always Christ will be honored in my body, whether by life or by death. For to me to live is Christ, and to die is gain" (Philippians 1:18b–21).

- Again, drawing on the same hope of the resurrection that awaits all Christians, Paul says to the Corinthians: "So we are always of *good courage*. We know that while we are at home in the body we are away from the Lord, for we walk by faith, not by sight. Yes, we are of *good courage*, and we would rather be away from the body and at home with the Lord" (2 Corinthians 5:6–8).

Παράκλησις (*Paraklesis*)

Beyond a command to take courage, there's plenty of scriptural talk about encouragement. First is the Greek verb *parakaleo*, which means "to call near." Second is the Greek noun *paraklesis*, which is often translated "encouragement." It's an encouragement that comes from the call to faith, the work of the Spirit who "calls, gathers, enlightens, and sanctifies the whole Christian church on earth" (Small Catechism, Third Article). It's why Jesus calls the Holy Spirit the *Paraclete*, the Comforter.

- St. Paul wrote to the Philippians: "So if there is any *encouragement* in Christ, any comfort from love, any participation in the Spirit, any affection and sympathy, complete my joy by being of the same mind, having the same love, being in full accord and of one mind" (Philippians 2:1–2).

- And he wrote to the Romans: "For whatever was written in former days was written for our instruction, that through endurance and through the *encouragement* of the Scriptures we might have hope. May the God of endurance and *encouragement* grant you to live in such harmony with one another, in accord with Christ Jesus, that together you may with one voice glorify the God and Father of our Lord Jesus Christ" (Romans 15:4–6).

- The author of Hebrews wrote: "So when God desired to show more convincingly to the heirs of the promise the unchangeable character of His purpose, He guaranteed it with an oath, so that by two unchangeable things, in which it is impossible for God to lie, we who have fled for refuge might have *strong encouragement* to hold fast to the hope set before us" (Hebrews 6:17–18).

- Luke explains that the name Barnabas means "son of *encouragement*" (Acts 4:36).

Courage is a potent theme throughout the New Testament. Why? Two reasons. One, we are prone to discouragement. Our sinful flesh wants to shy away from the fight, shirk the calling to confess Christ with confidence. And two, if the resurrection of Jesus from the dead is true, and if we share in His death and resurrection through our Baptism into Him, we have an undaunted courage to face whatever trials and difficulties await us. Nothing can unbaptize us. God makes an eternal promise to us there. Our resurrection is rock-solid certain. Therefore, *take courage!*

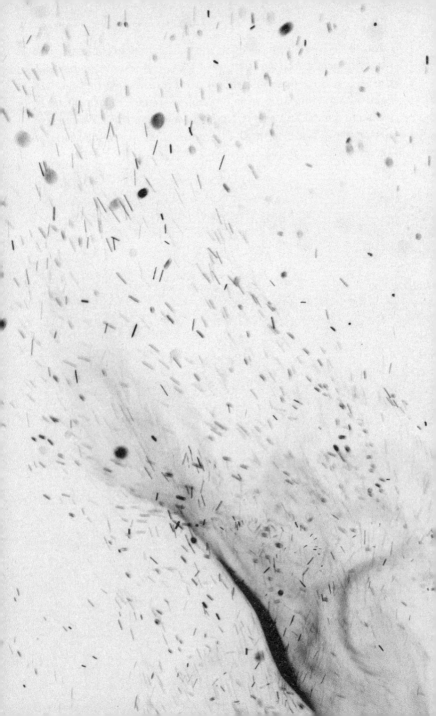

PART I

Courage to Live

· ·

The rules have changed. Going to church was once as normal as brushing your hair; now it is as normal as brushing your hat. Words and actions that were polite twenty or even ten years ago have become offensive, and trying to opt out of bizarre demands is incriminating. ("Silence is violence!")

If you can't win, why play? But life isn't a game. Martin Luther's Morning Prayer has the Christian ask God each morning "that all my doings and life may please You." Life is a gift and duty we receive from the Lord.

Christians seek to live by the Ten Commandments, comforted by God's Word and His promise to hear us and strengthened by the Sacraments. This means we approach each day's claims on us with immeasurably more guidance and help than those whom we may find threatening.

You are a child of the living God. So don't be afraid to live!

Seek Ye First

....

"Do not be anxious," says Jesus (Matthew 6:25). Why? God takes care of the birds, doesn't He? And you are far more valuable. Won't He take care of you? Your worry will not add an hour to your life (Matthew 6:27). Don't worry about clothing. Why? The lilies are here today and gone tomorrow, and they are more glorious than the great King Solomon in all his splendor (Luke 12:27). Won't your heavenly Father clothe you? Are you worried about food and drink? Why? Your Father knows you need these things. Hasn't He always provided them?

But seek first the kingdom of God and His righteousness, and all these things will be added to you. (Matthew 6:33)

When Jesus first preached on this earth, He cried, "Repent, for the kingdom of heaven is at hand" (Matthew 4:17). Jesus is Himself the kingdom of God, and He delivers Himself to us through His Word, as we learned in the catechism:

The kingdom of God certainly comes by itself without our prayer, but we pray in this petition that it may come to us also.

How does God's kingdom come? **God's kingdom comes when our heavenly Father gives us His Holy Spirit, so that by His grace we believe His holy Word and lead godly lives here in time and there in eternity.** (Small Catechism, Second Petition)

This promise helps us face our anxieties and cry out in confidence to our Lord and Savior. In His Word, He teaches us to pray.

- *I'm anxious!* You bore on the cross all the anxiety of the world. Lord, continue to slay my anxiety, and give me Your Spirit.

- *I'm discontented!* You, Lord, carried my anxieties to Golgotha. Lord, forgive my sin.

- *I'm jealous!* Lord, slay my sinful flesh by Your word of Law, and give me Your kingdom anew by Your Gospel. Cause me to rejoice in the blessings You give to others.

- *I'm worried!* All worry was subsumed and sentenced to death when You said, "It is finished" (John 19:30). Lord, grant me contentment in You and Your promises.

- *I'm greedy and self-centered!* You, Lord, gave Yourself totally, for the totality of my sin. Create in me a clean heart and renew my feeble spirit (Psalm 51:10).

- *I'm afraid to confess Your name!* You, Lord, confessed before Pilate. You confessed Psalm 22 on the cross. Strengthen my feeble knees and open my lips, and my mouth will praise Your name "to a people yet unborn" (Psalm 22:31).

O blessed Jesus, I seek Your kingdom. O Jesus, I seek Your righteousness. For Your sake, I pray with St. Paul:

> **I have suffered the loss of all things and count them as rubbish, in order that I may gain Christ and be found in Him, not having a righteousness of my own that comes from the law, but that which comes through faith in Christ, the righteousness from God that depends on faith—that I may know Him and the power of His resurrection, and may share His sufferings, becoming like Him in His death, that by any means possible I may attain the resurrection from the dead.** (Philippians 3:8–11)

Lord, take my anxiousness and grant me faith in Your fatherly divine goodness and mercy through Jesus Christ. Grant to me Your kingdom, Your righteousness, and render me content with Your blessings.

Amen, Amen.

Christian Certainty

Our heavenly Father is pleased when a Christian is absolutely certain of His love and forgiveness now, certain of eternal life with Him upon death, and certain of a bodily resurrection like Christ's own at the Last Day. In the face of all the bad stuff happening to him at the hands of people and of God, Job confesses with absolute certainty:

> Oh that my words were written! Oh that they were inscribed in a book! Oh that with an iron pen and lead they were engraved in the rock forever! For I know that my Redeemer lives, and at the last He will stand upon the earth. And after my skin has been thus destroyed, yet in my flesh I shall see God, whom I shall see for myself, and my eyes shall behold, and not another. My heart faints within me! (Job 19:23–27)

I want to encourage you to be certain. Christ's Gospel is absolutely certain. This Christ was slain from the foundation of the world for you. He knows who you are; He knows your name. He knows the town you work in. He knows your vocation; He's given it to you. He knows your family; He knows every difficulty you face; He knows all your weaknesses. And He's placed you where He's placed you. He's given you sacred vocations to fulfill, service to the church and your community. He knows you're imperfect. That's why He's perfect.

You have certain commandments, the Ten Commandments. They are absolutely clear. *You shall not.* They damn us all. That's why we in the Church should not spend most of our time looking outside and condemning the culture, condemning the people around us, condemning others. Most of our time speaking the Law in the Church needs to be speaking the Law to ourselves. When Jesus said,

"You brood of vipers," to whom was He talking (see Matthew 12:34; 23:33)? He was talking to the religious people. They were the people in church. That applies to all of us: *You brood of vipers.* You and I commit sins, and not even occasionally. When our hands and our feet do the right thing, when our mouths say the right thing, our minds are full of absolute stench and filth. We hate. We're envious. We're prideful. We're unforgiving. Think of the person in your family who's the black sheep, or how your heart is inclined negatively toward people who've harmed you in the past. Jesus says that if you hate somebody, that's murder (1 John 3:15). The Law damns us completely (Romans 3:11–12). And it's absolutely clear. It also gives us a clear path for living. It's certain.

The Law is given to all. Its chief purpose is to drive us to repentance. It is given, says St. Paul, "that every mouth may be stopped, and the whole world may be held accountable to God. For by works of the law no human being will be justified in His sight, since through the law comes knowledge of sin" (Romans 3:19–20).

The Law is but a mirror bright
To bring the inbred sin to light. (*LSB* 555:3)

Christ came for sinners. You are one. There's no gray here. "None is righteous. No, not one" (Romans 3:10). The Law condemns because we do not meet its demands. The Law drives us to Jesus, who met all its demands (Romans 5:19) and died to put its punishments to death (atonement, Romans 5:9).

The Creed is absolutely certain. The First Article (Creation) teaches that this world and all its inhabitants are God's precious creation and creatures. It is certain. Our heavenly Father is the source of all that we are, have, and enjoy. The Second Article (Redemption) teaches with all biblical certainty that Christ "has redeemed me . . . not with gold or silver, but with His holy, precious blood and with His innocent suffering and death" (Small Catechism, Second Article; see 1 Peter 1:18–19). It's absolutely certain that Jesus really did die. Suffered under Pontius Pilate, crucified, dead, and buried. Descended into hell. Proclaimed victory. Raised and ascended into heaven to sit at the right hand of God the Father Almighty. The deed was done already 2,000 years ago. The Gospel is yours. It's absolutely certain. Why did the apostles all die violent deaths? Because they knew Jesus rose from the grave. They had seen Him alive themselves. And they were His witnesses. They were compelled to preach it! (See 1 Corinthians 9:16.) It's certain. It's absolutely certain.

The Third Article (Sanctification) teaches us: "I believe that I cannot . . . believe in Jesus Christ, my Lord, or come to Him; but the Holy Spirit has called me by the Gospel" (Small Catechism, Third Article). My salvation is certain because it's not won by me, not worked by me, not decided by me (John 15:16), not preserved by me. It's all God's working, beginning to end. It's an "inheritance that is imperishable, undefiled, and unfading, kept in heaven for you, who by God's power are being guarded through faith" (1 Peter 1:4–5).

The Lord's Prayer is absolutely certain. You are given the Lord's very words. Jesus promised His apostles: "Whatever you ask in My name, this I will do" (John 14:13). Jesus invites us to pray to Him: "Come to Me, all who labor and are heavy laden, and I will give you rest" (Matthew 11:28). Jesus teaches us the very words to pray in the Lord's Prayer: "Our Father who art in heaven." (See Matthew 6:9–13; Luke 11:2–4.) Luther writes: "With these words God tenderly invites us to believe that He is our true Father and that we are His true children, so that with all boldness and confidence [certainty!] we may ask Him as dear children ask their dear father" (Small Catechism, Lord's Prayer, Introduction). So Jesus says, "This is My Father, and now I want *you* to call Him Father." Isn't that the most marvelous thing? These petitions are what Jesus wants you to pray. And He promises that, for His sake, your Father hears them and answers them for you, for your good. It's certain.

You have Baptism. It's absolutely certain. By being baptized, Jesus put Himself into Baptism. Jesus mandated Baptism, saying that through Baptism disciples are made of all nations (Matthew 28:19). He also taught: "Whoever believes and is baptized will be saved" (Mark 16:16). The apostles repeatedly taught that Baptism is a saving act, for it connects us with Christ's death, burial, and His resurrection (Colossians 2:6–15; Romans 6). "He saved us through the washing of rebirth and renewal by the Holy Spirit" (Small Catechism, Baptism; see Titus 3:5–8). Baptism is the forgiveness of sins. Baptism is justification. Baptism *is* the Gospel. It's certain.

You are baptized. The Bible says we are buried with Christ in Baptism (Romans 6:3–4). Baptism connects us with Jesus (Colossians 2:12). It's not a symbol. It truly does it. "Baptism . . . now saves you" (1 Peter 3:21). It delivers the goods. You are forgiven. It renders your conscience clean (Hebrews 10:22). Jesus is for sinners, only for sinners. And you happen to be one. There's a nice fit. You'd better always be a sinner because Jesus comes for sinners. Absolutely certain.

And you are absolved. Your pastor absolves you. Your sins are forgiven. Why confess our sins to a pastor privately and at the beginning of the Divine Service? Because Jesus mandated it. "He breathed on [His disciples] and said to them . . . 'If you forgive the sins of any, they are forgiven them'" (John 20:22–23). Jesus said it. Jesus gave it. Faith receives it. It is the Gospel. It is certain. In fact, "this is just as valid and certain, even in heaven, as if Christ our dear Lord dealt with us Himself" (Small Catechism, Confession). It's also meant to open our lips to speak the Gospel of forgiveness to those in our lives.

And the Sacrament is yours, the body and blood of Christ. It's absolutely certain. It's His very body and blood for you, given and shed for you. For what? For the forgiveness of sins. Jesus says, "Take, eat; this is My body. . . . Drink of it, all of you; this cup is . . . My blood, which is shed for you for the forgiveness of sins" (Small Catechism, Sacrament of the Altar). (Those who assert that "this is My body" actually means "this is not really My body" forever have the burden of explaining why Jesus did not mean what He said.) Jesus' words are clear and very certain. We receive the gift believing Christ's words. And it is absolutely certain. "Whoever feeds on My flesh and drinks My blood has eternal life, and I will raise him up on the last day" (John 6:54).

The Lord gives His Gospel to us in manifold ways. Salvation was earned on the cross and is distributed by the proclaimed Word of the Gospel, Absolution, Baptism, and the Lord's Supper. That certainty is more than we need in these crazy times to hold our heads high and say: "Come, Lord Jesus" and "Come what may." I *know* that my Redeemer lives (Job 19:25). All this He has given so that I may be absolutely certain that I am His baptized child now and that I shall enjoy the resurrection of my flesh, with Him and all the saints, into eternity (1 Corinthians 15).

Let Not Your Hearts Be Troubled[1]

. . . .

The Helper, the Holy Spirit, whom the Father will send in My name, He will teach you all things and bring to your remembrance all that I have said to you. Peace I leave with you; My peace I give to you. Not as the world gives do I give to you. Let not your hearts be troubled, neither let them be afraid. (John 14:26–27)

I suspect that you and I have something very much in common. I have had quite enough of the endless talk of the coronavirus—on Facebook, in every form of communication, on every minute of talk radio, on every second of television, radio, and all other forms of news. I've had enough of the scenarios repeated over and over again—the prognostications, the predictions, the revisions of predictions, the predicted revisions, and even the public service announcements.

I've had it with the political shoving matches and fights over who did what when—over respirators and ventilators and masks and chloroquine and plasma treatments. Yes, it works, or it may work; or no, it doesn't work. Is there a vaccine on the way? Yes and no. The infection rate is very high! No, the infection rate is actually very low. It really only affects the older folks and those with pre-morbid conditions. ("Pre-morbid"—that was a new one on me!) No, young people are in fact dying and suffering horribly. And where did it come from?

---

1   This is an edited version of a sermon that originally aired on *The Lutheran Hour* in 2020. Used with permission of Lutheran Hour Ministries.

What's an essential service? Which businesses should be open? Which should be closed? Are liquor stores essential and churches nonessential? Who says so? The mayor? The county commissioner? The governor? The federal government? Why are the same guidelines interpreted differently by authorities in different communities? Where are the boundaries between government authority and religious liberty? Can First Amendment rights be surrendered? How can a church and its pastor carefully obtain permission from the local authorities to have limited services, with limited numbers of people, with all the social distancing required . . . and then still be subject to harassment and even death threats?

When should we start opening the country again? Has the peak been reached? Has it passed? Have many more been infected than we thought and thus developed antibodies? Are we risking more waves of infection? Will the economy come back? Is the damage irreversible? Will this epidemic change the way we look at social interaction—the way we look at church and school and medicine and work and government and a hundred other things?

What a baffling, babbling cacophony of contradictory craziness! Yes, babbling!

It's Pentecost. Jesus has something to say just for you, and Jesus doesn't babble: "Don't be afraid."

There are three texts from the Bible that the church often reads on Pentecost Sunday. The first comes from the earliest part of the Bible. Genesis 11 tells the short story of the tower of Babel. Details are disappointingly few. Somewhere near what today would be modern Iraq, the descendants of Noah—long ago, sometime after the great flood—decided to build themselves a great tower. It appears they had a new construction technique, and they were very proud of what they had achieved and were planning to do. They said, "Let us make a name for ourselves" (Genesis 11:4). But they had forgotten the Lord God. God responded by "confusing their language" and spreading them around the earth. They could no longer understand one another and complete their massive construction project. Their great plan was foiled! That's where we get the words "babble," "babbling," and "babbler." It all comes from the tower of "Babel."

Dissension, disunity, disharmony, confusion, conflict—even the inability to understand one another's languages—are all the result of sin and its punishment. But Jesus came to de-confuse, to de-babble Babel.

In fact, Jesus spoke *very* clearly. He tells us some great things in the Pentecost Gospel from John. He was talking to His disciples just before He was betrayed:

> **If anyone loves Me, he will keep My word, and My Father will love him, and We will come to him and make Our home with him. Whoever does not love Me does not keep My words. And the word that you hear is not Mine but the Father's who sent Me.** (John 14:23–24)

Jesus says, "Hold on to My word." Grab it! That's what faith does!

Jesus made a promise in this last speech to His disciples: "These things I have spoken to you while I am still with you. But the Helper, the Holy Spirit, whom the Father will send in My name, He will teach you all things and bring to your remembrance all that I have said to you" (John 14:25–26).

Then on Pentecost, the promised Holy Spirit descended upon the apostles. The Spirit brought to memory all the things that Jesus had said to them so they could speak them and write them down in the Gospels. "Peace I leave with you; My peace I give to you. Not as the world gives do I give to you. Let not your hearts be troubled, neither let them be afraid!" (John 14:27).

And Jesus even undid Babel! The Bible tells us in Acts 2 that the apostles, filled with the Holy Spirit, speak so that "Parthians and Medes and Elamites, residents of Mesopotamia, Judea and Cappadocia, Pontus and Asia, Phrygia and Pamphylia, Egypt and the parts of Libya belonging to Cyrene, and visitors from Rome, both Jews and proselytes, Cretans and Arabians . . . hear [in their] own tongues the mighty works of God" (vv. 9–11).

With the gift of the Holy Spirit, making his words heard by all—un-babbling the babble of Babel—Peter preached it! Folks from all over the world heard Peter's sermon that day, each in his own language. They all witnessed the fulfillment of Joel's prophecy, that the Spirit would be poured out on all flesh (Joel 2:28–29). From that time until this very moment, the apostles and Christ's Church have continued the preaching of Jesus Himself. "Repent, for the kingdom of heaven is at hand!" (Matthew 3:2). Be sorry for your sins and believe in Jesus, who has paid your price by His death and overcome your sin and your death by His resurrection! Don't be afraid! In fact, on this Pentecost Day, these words I speak are the very words of Jesus, accompanied by the power of the Holy Spirit, and they are addressed to you, right now, as I speak them. Jesus' words to you hold good, no matter what comes next in this crazy world! Jesus doesn't give you pseudo-religious nonsense. He's got the remedy for Babel, and He doesn't babble. It's crystal clear.

"Peace I leave with you; My peace I give to you. Not as the world gives do I give to you. Let not your hearts be troubled, neither let them be afraid" (John 14:27). Jesus has grabbed hold of you with these words.

I Challenge You
to Read Your Bible

··

Friedrich Pfotenhauer was president of The Lutheran Church—
Missouri Synod from 1911 to 1935. In 1897, on the fiftieth
anniversary of the Synod, he was president of the Minnesota and
Dakota District. He said the following to the gathered district
pastors and laypeople:

> Finally, we have cause to celebrate our synodical jubilee
> with fear and trembling when we glance at the present con-
> dition of our Synod. *It is true, we still have the very precious
> treasure, the pure Word of God.* As a rule, it still governs
> our congregations, but it cannot be denied that we are no
> longer what our fathers were. Indeed, *the symptoms of the
> decline are evident and increasing among us. I will only point
> out a few. The holy zeal to study and grow in God's Word has
> declined markedly among both preachers and hearers.*
>
> *The boundary between us and the world is no longer drawn
> so sharply.* Our manner of life is not always prudent.
> Terrible scandals, also on the part of our pastors, are on
> the increase. While we are richer in earthly things than our
> fathers, we are weaker in faith and Christian love.[1]

Wow! If Pfotenhauer felt that way about his generation, I daresay
his words are an indictment exponentially greater upon ours. We
spend plenty of time lamenting the state of the world, but we have

---

1 *At Home in the House of My Fathers*, ed. Matthew C. Harrison (St. Louis: Concordia Publishing House, 2011), 714 (emphasis added).

a much more difficult time recognizing the encroachment of the world's viewpoints upon us.

Jesus preached, *Back to the Bible!* "You search the Scriptures because you think that in them you have eternal life; and it is they that bear witness about Me" (John 5:39). The apostles preached, *Back to the Bible!* In fact, every great era of reform in the Church's life has begun with the cry to repentance and *Back to the Bible!*

The Lutheran Reformation was exactly such an event. The Lutheran Confessional Revival of the nineteenth century was also such an event. After a century of pastors and scholars denying that the Scriptures are the Word of God—and even that Christ is the God-man, "the Lamb of God who takes away the sin of the world" (John 1:29)—a revival of serious study of the Word of God began in the 1820s. Soon, many were captivated by the truth of Scripture. In Germany, after people began reading the Word again, they read the Lutheran Confessions and came to the joyful discovery that the Confessions agree with the Word. Those who confessed this were themselves, in fact, Lutheran. This happened to many of the great founders of the LCMS, including C. F. W. Walther, Friedrich Wyneken, Wilhelm Sihler, and Wilhelm Loehe.

The Scriptures are God's own inspired and infallible Word. "Holy men of God [spoke] as they were moved by the Holy [Spirit]" (2 Peter 1:21 KJV). Jesus Himself quoted the Old Testament as the very Word of God, absolutely reliable and authoritative ("the mouth of God," Matthew 4:4; "It is written," Matthew 21:13, Mark 11:17, Luke 19:46; "this that is written must yet be accomplished in Me," Luke 22:37 KJV; "have [you] not read that which was spoken unto you by God" Matthew 22:31–32 KJV; and much more!). *Back to the Bible!*

- Can we be sure of Christ, forgiveness, and eternal life? *Back to the Bible!* (1 John 4:1–4)

- How shall we treat each other in the Church? *Back to the Bible!* (1 Corinthians 13)

- Shall we share the Word of the Gospel with others? *Back to the Bible!* (Luke 19:10)

- How shall we hold up under suffering and ill health? *Back to the Bible!* (Romans 5; Hebrews 12; 1 Peter 1)

There is no problem of faith, life, family, or church for which the Bible does not have answers. If you're looking for a place to start, check out *The Lutheran Study Bible*, available from Concordia Publishing House. In the preface material, you'll find helpful tools such as "How to Read and Study the Bible" and a two-year plan for reading through the whole Bible. Four chapters a day gets you through the whole Bible in two years. I have an app on my iPhone which allows me to listen to the Scriptures while I'm in the car or at the gym.

Are you worried about the present condition of our Synod? Have you observed that the symptoms of the decline are evident and increasing among us? Do you wonder if the holy zeal to study and grow in God's Word has declined markedly among both preachers and hearers? Does it bother you that the boundary between us and the world is no longer drawn so sharply? Isn't it obvious that, while we are richer in earthly things than our fathers, we are weaker in faith and Christian love?

If these are your questions, you are in the good company of Pastor Pfotenhauer in 1897. But there is another thing that has remained the same between his time and ours: *It is true, we still have the very precious treasure, the pure Word of God.* One little word can fell every enemy of Christ and His Church, and we know where to find that Word. *Back to the Bible!* I challenge you!

God's Clear,
Reliable Word

....

O urs is a day of tremendous ignorance, particularly about the
Bible and the Christian faith. Foolish and ignorant views
about the Bible and its message abound. We have heard many
times that the Bible has allegedly been translated so many times
into different languages that the original text has been lost, and
no one actually knows what it was or what it means.

In fact, we have more reliable ancient manuscripts of the Bible in
its original languages (Hebrew, Aramaic, and Greek) than any other
ancient literature. The books of the New Testament were carefully
copied and spread throughout the ancient Mediterranean world and
beyond. Any errors scribes made in copying are overwhelmingly identifiable: they result from misunderstandings in speaking or hearing
while one person read the text and several copied, or perhaps when
a scribe tried to "fix" a New Testament text that seemed difficult to
understand or to harmonize it with another text. These are easily
identifiable, especially because loads of other manuscripts uniformly
express the original. A couple of sections of the Gospels are not in all
the ancient versions (such as the long ending of Mark), but there is
no Christian doctrine that depends only on these few texts.

The Old Testament Hebrew text is amazingly reliable. Prior to
the discovery of the Dead Sea Scrolls in 1946–47, the Church relied
upon a Hebrew text from the ninth or tenth century. All of a sudden,
archaeologists found manuscripts a thousand years older, including
many whole books of the Old Testament, plus many smaller fragments.
The Dead Sea texts and the manuscripts from a millennium later are
nearly identical. Ancient Jewish copyists ensured this accuracy by

counting letters from the front and back of Old Testament sections of books (e.g., the Torah, or first five books of Moses, or the Psalms). If the numerical center of the manuscript did not land on a certain letter of a certain verse, the manuscript was removed from use.

When we confess the "verbal inspiration" of the Bible in all matters, and thus the "inerrancy" of Scripture, we confess this most precisely about the original manuscripts that came from the hands of the prophets, apostles, or their secretaries. That doesn't mean there are not challenges and difficulties, some of which may not be solved in this life. We trust the Holy Spirit, who knows more than we do, or assume some scribe made a mistake in copying. And remember, any time you find such a rare problem in the Bible, some 2,000 years of Christians have already dealt with the problem.

The teachings of the Christian faith are, in fact, quite clear. They are found in extremely clear, uncontested biblical texts. For example, every statement of the Apostles' Creed is linked to clear texts, and most often *many* clear texts. *Luther's Small Catechism with Explanation* (2017) builds on these clear teachings of Scripture. This updated edition teaches God's Word especially well and includes more verses of Scripture than any catechism in the history of the Synod!

I recently asked members of my own parish how many had the new catechism from The Lutheran Church—Missouri Synod and Concordia Publishing House. I was amazed at how few did. Luther's catechism proper (the Six Chief Parts) provides the strong doctrine-laden texts that make clear the basics, without which a person cannot be a Christian (Ten Commandments, Apostles' Creed, Lord's Prayer, Baptism, Confession, Lord's Supper). The explanation provides hundreds of crystal-clear texts that teach every aspect of the faith: the justification of the sinner before God; who God is, Father, Son, and Holy Spirit; who Jesus is as God and man; the Sacraments; the Church; what is a pastor. It also addresses challenging ethical issues we face today such as marital problems, racism, abortion, drug abuse, giving to those in need, and much more. Get the new catechism. In fact, get a stack of them for everyone in your congregation. Make them available to all members to share with their family and friends.

I was in Nebraska recently for their district convention. An older farmer pulled me aside and said, "Pastor, I have to tell you something."

"What's that?"

"Pastor, I see people, young people, hurting or confused." He began tearing up. "I know it when I see 'em, Pastor. I know they're hurting. You know what I do, Pastor? I give them a catechism."

"Oh," I said. "You give them the little pamphlet edition of Luther's Catechism, just Luther's part?"

"No, Pastor. I give 'em the whole thing. You wouldn't believe what happens." He proceeded to tell me amazing things that happened in the life of the recipients: conversions to Lutheranism, fresh comfort from the Word, and consolation in the midst of struggles.

Last week I went to Concordia Publishing House, and I bought a stack of catechisms. Before I got home that day, I gave away three—two to people looking for a church that teaches the Word of God.

"How can I, unless someone guides me?" the Ethiopian eunuch asked Philip (Acts 8:31). Philip had asked the man if he understood the Scripture he was reading. We often have the same question. It's vital to know the clear and main teachings of the Bible to be able to read it most profitably. That's what the Small Catechism is and does. It's nothing but the Bible. That's why Luther translated the New Testament so early in the Reformation (and continued on to translate the Old Testament as well); it's why he wrote the Small Catechism and Large Catechism in 1529. The Small Catechism is our Philip.

Read your Bible. Read it daily. Read your catechism. Read it daily. Buy your kids and grandkids the new catechism. Get *The Lutheran Study Bible*. Buy your kids Bible story books from Concordia Publishing House (cph.org). God works through His Holy Word (including the texts in the Small Catechism) to create faith in those who hear and read it. "So shall My word be that goes out from My mouth; it shall not return to Me empty" (Isaiah 55:11). Knowing the Word of God will make you confident in your salvation, wrought by Christ and pointed to by the whole Bible.

Incarnation
and Certainty
about the Word

....

Jesus made many outlandish claims about Himself, none more outrageous than that He is God in the flesh: "I and the Father are one" (John 10:30).

The religious leaders repeatedly charged Jesus with blasphemy because of this. Jesus invited divine worship of Himself (John 9:35–38). Thomas, praising Jesus from his knees, called Him "My Lord and my God!" (John 20:28). While He walked the earth, Jesus did divine things: "Who can forgive sins but God alone?" (Luke 5:21). "Who then is this, that even the wind and the sea obey Him?" (Mark 4:41). He shed divine/human blood to pay for the sins of the world: "Behold, the Lamb of God, who takes away the sin of the world!" (John 1:29). "The blood of Jesus His Son cleanses us from all sin" (1 John 1:7). Yet He looked like an average Palestinian Jew and did everything a person does. He grew and learned, demonstrated emotions including anger and frustration, suffered pain, endured sickness (Isaiah 53:2–4), said and did inexplicable things, which sometimes appeared contradictory and confusing.

> When many of His disciples heard it, they said, "This is a hard saying; who can listen to it?" . . . Many of His disciples turned back and no longer walked with Him. (John 6:60, 66)

"For we do not have a high priest who is unable to sympathize with our weaknesses, but one who in every respect has been tempted as we are, yet without sin" (Hebrews 4:15). Jesus is the sinless Son of

God, God in human flesh. Yet during His earthly life, many found Him confusing, contradictory. At times they even thought He was not only in error, but crazy or demonic. Some of His recorded statements continue to puzzle even the most pious, orthodox Christians. But no orthodox Christian will ever accuse Jesus of error, much less sin.

The incarnation of Christ provides us a guide or lens to look at Holy Scripture. The Scriptures are both divine—inspired by God and without error—while also being thoroughly human. They were written by sinful human authors who were inspired by the Holy Spirit. They wrote in different styles, including a more common Greek (John) and a more academic style (Hebrews). They wrote in Greek, Aramaic, and Hebrew, and in poetic, narrative, and other types of writing. Much of their writing is easy to understand, though some statements are difficult to understand or even confusing (like some of Jesus' own statements). The Scriptures themselves tell us about the theological errors of St. Peter that St. Paul corrected (Galatians 2:11–21). Peter himself is an author of Holy Scripture. But it's also Peter who wrote of Holy Scripture: "Men spoke from God as they were carried along by the Holy Spirit" (2 Peter 1:21).

In fact, St. Peter includes the prophetic witness of the apostles about Jesus and the Old Testament when he writes:

> For we did not follow cleverly devised myths when we made known to you the power and coming of our Lord Jesus Christ, but we were eyewitnesses of His majesty. For when He received honor and glory from God the Father, and the voice was borne to Him by the Majestic Glory, "This is My beloved Son, with whom I am well pleased," we ourselves heard this very voice borne from heaven, for we were with Him on the holy mountain. And we have the prophetic word more fully confirmed, to which you will do well to pay attention as to a lamp shining in a dark place, until the day dawns and the morning star rises in your hearts, knowing this first of all, that no prophecy of Scripture comes from someone's own interpretation. For no prophecy was ever produced by the will of man, but

men spoke from God as they were carried along by the Holy Spirit. (2 Peter 1:16–21)

Here, Peter simply repeats Jesus' own view of the Scriptures, which the Savior Himself said "bear witness about Me" and thus save (John 5:39), are without error (John 10:35), and come directly from God (Mark 7:13; Matthew 4:4; Matthew 21:13; Mark 11:17; Luke 19:46).

We absolutely do *not* begin our witness to someone by attempting to prove the Scriptures are true, Genesis 1 to Revelation 22, and without error or contradiction, as though only then could a person trust in Christ as Savior. We proclaim Christ and His precious Gospel, the full forgiveness of sins acquired on the cross, and the world-acquitting act of His resurrection (Romans 4:24–25). "Faith comes from hearing, and hearing through the word of Christ" (Romans 10:17). Once a person is brought by the Word of Christ's Gospel to believe in the Savior, that person recognizes the voice of his Savior in Holy Scripture. The great president of both the LCMS and Concordia Seminary Franz Pieper (1852–1931) put it beautifully:

> In dealing with an unbeliever we cannot begin with an attempt to convince him of the divine authority of Scripture. We must first bring him to the knowledge of his sins and to faith in Christ, the Redeemer from sin. We should preach to him on the basis of Scripture—without discussing the authority of Scripture—repentance and remission of sin. If a man has in this way—and there is no other way—become a Christian . . . then he will know that the Word of Scripture is God's Word, just as the children of God among the Jews knew and received the word Christ spoke as God's Word.[1]

Holy Scripture is God's own divine/human Word. Just like Luther, who spent a lifetime studying the Scriptures and scratching his head over challenging texts, we will find things that sound like mistakes

---

1   *Christian Dogmatics*, trans. Theodore Engelder et al. (St. Louis: Concordia Publishing House, 1950), 1:137.

and contradictions in the Bible. But these are a result of our limited human understanding, not of errors in the Word. It's great comfort to know Jesus' view of the Bible and also to know that Christians from the beginning have wrestled with the very same texts. Most difficulties melt away with good instruction: the assistance of a pastor, the guidance of *The Lutheran Study Bible*, or insight from a reliable commentary. Some texts will cause us to scratch our heads, perhaps until the resurrection. In such cases, with Luther, we'll "doff our hat to the Holy Spirit, knowing He's a better theologian than we are." Like the divinity/humanity of Christ, so also the divine/human nature of the inerrant and infallible Scriptures will remain an article of faith, not sight.

Fear Not the Foe

uther often commented that the devil cannot stand to be ridiculed. Our newest hymnal, *Lutheran Service Book*, puts a belly laugh right in the devil's face by choosing to place "O Little Flock, Fear Not the Foe" as hymn number 666. This strong little song depicts the Church on earth—the Church Militant—confident in the face of growing opposition.

> O little flock, fear not the foe
> Who madly seeks your overthrow;
> Dread not his rage and pow'r.
> And though your courage sometimes faints,
> His seeming triumph o'er God's saints
> Lasts but a little hour. (*LSB* 666:1)

The birth of our Savior wondrously illustrates the truth this hymn expresses. The King of all creation comes to this world as a lowly child, born of a young virgin in an animal stable. The person in whom all time and eternity meet, "very God of very God" (Nicene Creed)—"begotten of the Father from eternity, and also true man, born of the Virgin Mary" (Small Catechism, Second Article)—was laid in a manger. Herod gets word that there's a new king in town and "madly seeks" His "overthrow." The birth of this little babe prompts a mad rage by the powerful, the preferred, the establishment.

> Be of good cheer; your cause belongs
> To Him who can avenge your wrongs;
> Leave it to Him, our Lord.
> Though hidden yet from mortal eyes,
> His Gideon shall for you arise,
> Uphold you and His Word. (*LSB* 666:2)

Christ's glory was hidden, even as He was revealed—from the flight to Egypt to His boyhood in Nazareth; from a humble Baptism by John (who was shocked that the Savior of the world would seek Baptism from him) to temptation in the wilderness; to preaching repentance and the Good News; to the opposition of the leaders of Israel; to plots to confound and kill Him; to suffering in the garden, betrayal, capture, trial on false charges; to conviction by a mere mortal; to crucifixion; to ridicule even on the cross; to last words and death. The Son of God's divinity flashed forth here and there—at His Baptism, at His transfiguration, in His miracles and miraculous words—but His glory was hidden. God's Word records this state of affairs in an upside-down way. "The hour has come for the Son of Man to be glorified," said Jesus, speaking of His very crucifixion (John 12:23). "Truly this man was the Son of God," said the Gentile centurion as he stared at the dead Savior (Mark 15:39).

And then, the glorious resurrection proved Jesus' life and words to be true. His resurrection was the great absolution of the sins of the world. "Be of good cheer; your cause belongs To Him who can avenge your wrongs; Leave it to Him, our Lord."

> As true as God's own Word is true,
> Not earth nor hell's satanic crew
> Against us shall prevail.
> Their might? A joke, a mere facade!
> God is with us and we with God—
> Our vict'ry cannot fail. (*LSB* 666:3)

The odds against the babe in the manger and the Christ on the cross were enormous, even absolute to any betting man. But there was something more than meets the eye. As Luther put it, if it were a mere man in the balance, over against the sins of the world, we'd be lost. But on the scale, over against our sins, is God in the flesh, and it's not even close. The "power" of sin? The "power" of the devil? The "power" of this world? The "power" of the flesh? "Their might? A joke, a mere facade! God is with us and we with God—Our vict'ry cannot fail."

> Amen, Lord Jesus, grant our prayer;
> Great Captain, now Thine arm make bare,
> Fight for us once again!

So shall Thy saints and martyrs raise
A mighty chorus to Thy praise
Forevermore. Amen. (*LSB* 666:4)

So much for this world's pomp and praise. So much for political folderol, losses and wins. So much for a vastly unchristian world. So much for all the worldly treasures and cares. So much for the odds. So much for the popular. So much for the fleeting worldly glory. So much for the odds against the Church. So much for the 666 and all that the beast can throw at Christ's "little flock." The prayer of the littlest child, "Come, Lord Jesus," is more powerful than all of that. Our "Great Captain" shall soon bare His arm. He waits to share the blessed Gospel with the last of the elect. "So shall" we with "Thy saints and martyrs raise A mighty chorus to Thy praise Forevermore. Amen."

O little flock, fear not the foe!

Does God Will Suffering and Affliction?

....

Does God will and even cause suffering? Or does He merely "allow" it to happen? Let's begin with the suffering and cross of Jesus. The answers to our questions about suffering, so far as we can understand anything at all of what the Bible teaches, begin and end with Jesus.

Did God know from eternity that the eternal Word, the Second Person of the Trinity, would assume flesh, be born, live, suffer, and die for the sins of the world? Certainly so. Revelation 13:8 calls Jesus "the Lamb slain from the foundation of the world" (KJV). Already at the fall into sin, God gave the promise: "He [the Christ] shall bruise your [Satan's] head, and you shall bruise His heel" (Genesis 3:15). The promise was repeated by the prophets, first to last, many times (Psalm 22; Isaiah 53). The lambs of Passover prefigured Christ. Did God will that those lambs be sacrificed and their blood mark the doors of the Hebrew people enslaved in Egypt? Quite certainly. He explicitly commanded that it be done (Exodus 12:7). When John the Baptizer pointed to Jesus and said, "Behold, the Lamb of God, who takes away the sin of the world" (John 1:29), was he indicating that the death of Jesus, though foreknown by God, would be effected by the will of men (for example, Judas, Pilate, religious leaders in Jerusalem)? No. There was more.

The answer comes most clearly in Gethsemane. "Father, if You are willing, remove this cup from Me. Nevertheless, not My will, but Yours, be done" (Luke 22:42). There it is. God the Father wills the suffering of God the Son. Under the pressure of the sins of the world, Jesus seemed to waver. Yet He, "who in every respect has been tempted as we are, yet without sin" (Hebrews 4:15), also did not sin at that tense moment. Jesus said, "No one takes [My life] from Me, but I lay it down of My own accord" (John 10:18).

There it is. God the Father and God the Son willed that the Son should suffer and die. God willed death. God willed suffering. At first, this is disconcerting. Isn't death a result of sin? Isn't suffering a result of sin? So, is God the cause of sin? No. God is not the cause and source of sin and death. Yet God Himself makes use of the curse of sin—suffering and death—for His good purposes. In doing so, He most often works in a hidden way. Our life is "hidden with Christ in God" (Colossians 3:3). Just think of it. As Christ was dying on the cross, His followers were terrified, distraught, hopeless, helpless. They thought that God had abandoned Jesus and *them*. But it was not so. The Father had abandoned Jesus to death *for them*. The greatest act in the history of the universe appeared to be the most pathetic, powerless, and useless failure.

Christians see the world differently. God used affliction to test Abraham by telling him to act contrary to His promise that the world would be blessed through Isaac (Genesis 22). God specifically gave Satan permission to all but slaughter Job (Job 1:6–12). Yet against all the evidence that God must hate him, Job replied in faith, "Though He slay me, I will hope in Him" (Job 13:15). St. Paul wrote:

> **A thorn was given me in the flesh, a messenger of Satan to harass me, to keep me from becoming conceited. . . . But He said to me, "My grace is sufficient for you, for My power is made perfect in weakness." Therefore I will boast all the more gladly of my weaknesses, so that the power of Christ may rest upon me.** (2 Corinthians 12:7, 9)

There are many such passages of God willing suffering for good, but all of them pale next to the cross. And the cross could only be understood after the resurrection.

What's God doing with COVID-19? One could suggest that sin somehow corrupted a perfect creation to cause some very harmful changes in microbes. St. Paul declares "that the whole creation has been groaning together in the pains of childbirth until now" (Romans 8:22). Our Lutheran forefathers, from Luther to C. F. W. Walther, never hesitated to preach that disasters and plagues were the just application of the Law upon the world and believers, to do what the Law always does, bring repentance.

Years ago, I was going through a particularly challenging period (what it was about, I do not recall). A dear colleague of mine pointed me to the following passage of our wonderful Lutheran Formula of Concord, confessed by all the congregations, pastors, and church workers in the LCMS. I've never been able to forget it:

> Furthermore, this doctrine [eternal election] provides glorious consolation under the cross and amid temptations. In other words, God in His counsel, before the time of the world, determined and decreed that He would assist us in all distresses [anxieties and perplexities]. He determined to grant patience [under the cross], give consolation, nourish and encourage hope, and produce an outcome for us that would contribute to our salvation. Also, Paul teaches this in a very consoling way. He explains that *God in His purpose has ordained before the time of the world by what crosses and sufferings He would conform every one of His elect to the image of His Son. His cross shall and must work together for good for everyone*, because they are called according to God's purpose. Therefore, Paul has concluded that it is certain and beyond doubt that neither "tribulation, or distress," neither "death nor life," or other such things "will be able to separate us from the love of God in Christ Jesus our Lord." (Solid Declaration of the Formula of Concord XI 48–49, emphasis added)

I cannot fully fathom the tiniest portion of what God is up to in times of crisis. I do know what He did in the cross of Jesus. I know that He knows what He is doing. I know that He works His greatest blessings through crosses. I plunge all my questions into the wounds of Christ on Calvary. I know that "He was pierced for our transgressions;

He was crushed for our iniquities . . . and with His wounds we are healed" (Isaiah 53:5). "But one of the soldiers pierced His side with a spear, and at once there came out blood and water" (John 19:34). I plunge my doubts into His hands and His side. I plunge my fears into His blood (in the Lord's Supper) and water (my precious Baptism). And I know that through crosses, the Father is conforming "every one of His elect to the image of His Son. His cross shall and must work together for good for everyone."

Courage
in the Darkness

· ·

Our world is completely unhinged. The evil that we hear of in the 24-hour news cycles, so often tragically affecting so many in our church body, is but a symptom of the chaos of these "gray and latter days." The political world is unhinged. The ethical world is unhinged. The social world is unhinged. The religious world is unhinged. The racial world is unhinged. The educational world is unhinged. The entertainment world is unhinged.

St. Paul saw it already and knew that it would get worse:

But understand this, that in the last days there will come times of difficulty. For people will be lovers of self, lovers of money, proud, arrogant, abusive, disobedient to their parents, ungrateful, unholy, heartless, unappeasable, slanderous, without self-control, brutal, not loving good, treacherous, reckless, swollen with conceit, lovers of pleasure rather than lovers of God, having the appearance of godliness, but denying its power. Avoid such people. For among them are those who creep into households and capture weak women, burdened with sins and led astray by various passions, always learning and never able to arrive at a knowledge of the truth. (2 Timothy 3:1–7)

And yet, there is a candle in the darkness. Like a lone paschal candle lit before Easter sunrise, the light of Christ is burning and the dawn of resurrection is glowing on the horizon. "Jesus spoke to them, saying, 'I am the light of the world. Whoever follows Me will not walk in darkness, but will have the light of life'" (John 8:12). And joyous wonder, as we look eastward for His return, Jesus brightens our faces even now, even as He pulls us out of darkness toward and into His marvelous light! He makes those who are His shine like Himself, for the sake of the lost.

> You are the light of the world. A city set on a hill cannot be hidden. Nor do people light a lamp and put it under a basket, but on a stand, and it gives light to all in the house. In the same way, let your light shine before others, so that they may see your good works and give glory to your Father who is in heaven. (Matthew 5:14–16)

In this same chapter of Matthew's Gospel, Jesus tells it like it now is and puts a surprisingly joyous spin on it:

> Blessed are you when others revile you and persecute you and utter all kinds of evil against you falsely on My account. Rejoice and be glad, for your reward is great in heaven, for so they persecuted the prophets who were before you. (Matthew 5:11–12)

And so I shall "rejoice and be glad." I shall not be burdened with anger and hatred. I shall confess it, and then I shall rejoice and be glad! In the face of fear and a myriad of pressures and challenges in the church, I shall rejoice and be glad. Luther said that the evil of original sin is so profound it can't be understood, but only believed; in the face of unspeakable and unfathomable evil, I shall "rejoice and be glad." And in this merciless world, marching to a funeral dirge because it does not yet know Christ, I shall, with St. Paul, sing Christ's name among those who don't yet know Him:

> "Therefore I will praise you among the Gentiles, and sing to Your name." And again it is said, "Rejoice, O Gentiles, with His people." (Romans 15:9–10)

> Because Christ has grabbed my heart and soul, my body and being;

> because He has brought me from darkness to light through Holy Baptism;

because He regularly forgives my sins anew in Holy Absolution;

because through my pastor He preaches forgiveness, peace, and joy into my ears and down to my soul;

because He consoles me by the words and Christian encouragement of brothers and sisters in the faith;

because He sets before me a feast of His very body and blood for my forgiveness . . . I shall be courageous and joyful.

From the Aaronic blessing at the end of the service until I return again for the trinitarian invocation, I shall march into my vocation as a light amid the darkness—as a sinner, to be sure, worn and torn, but glowing with Christ's own light.

I shall rejoice wherever the truth of Christ is known, whole or even in part, and yet I shall be fully Lutheran, for that is to be fully biblical.

May the God of hope fill you with all joy and peace in believing, so that by the power of the Holy Spirit you may abound in hope. (Romans 15:13)

Why Do We Suffer Trials?

. . . .

Luther famously wrote that there are three things that make a theologian (and this applies to all Christians). Taking his cue from King David in Psalm 119, Luther says: "There you will find three rules, amply presented throughout the whole Psalm. They are *Oratio* [prayer]; *Meditatio* [meditation on God's Word], *Tentatio* [trials]."[1] He then observed that the trials we experience really bring it all together. They drive us to rely on God's Word, and they drive us into prayer. He quipped, "I thank God for the pope. Through all his ranting and raving, he's made me a pretty good theologian."[2]

What is the purpose of trials in the Christian life? So often the afflictions of sin, death, and the devil are multiplied in the lives of Christians! Should we expect this? Jesus said, "If the world hates you, know that it has hated Me before it hated you" (John 15:18). It is also true that Christians often become more sensitive to their sins and shortcomings when they study what God's Word says about how serious their sins and shortcomings are. Trials are part of this trilogy that embeds faith in Christ deep in our being.

Oratio, Meditatio, Tentatio: Prayer, Meditation, Trial

The first part of Luther's trilogy is *prayer*.

Firstly, you should know that the Holy Scriptures constitute a book which turns the wisdom of all other books into

---

1   *Preface to Luther's German Writings*, AE 34:285.
2   See *Preface to Luther's German Writings*, AE 34:287.

foolishness, because not one teaches about eternal life except this one alone. . . . Kneel down in your little room [Matt. 6:6] and pray to God with real humility and earnestness, that he through his dear Son may give you his Holy Spirit, who will enlighten you, lead you, and give you understanding. Thus you see how David keeps praying . . . , "Teach me, Lord instruct me, lead me, show me."[3]

Such prayer is vital, and Luther knew that our prayers are most sure when we are praying as the Scriptures show us how to pray.

Second in Luther's trilogy is *meditation*:

Secondly, you should meditate, that is, not only in your heart, but also externally, by actually repeating and comparing oral speech and literal words of the book, reading and rereading them with diligent attention and reflection, so that you may see what the Holy Spirit means by them. And take care that you do not grow weary or think that you have done enough when you have read, heard, and spoken them once or twice, and that you then have complete understanding. You will never be a particularly good theologian if you do that, for you will be like untimely fruit which falls to the ground before it is half ripe. Thus you see in this same Psalm how David constantly boasts that he will talk, meditate, speak, sing, hear, read, by day and night and always, about nothing except God's Word and commandments. For God will not give you his Spirit without the external Word; so take your cue from that. His command to write, preach, read, hear, sing, speak, etc., outwardly was not in vain.[4]

Trials are third for Luther.

Thirdly, there is *tentatio, Anfechtung* [trials, spiritual attack]. This is the touchstone, which teaches you not only to know and understand, but also to experience how right, how true,

3   *Preface to Luther's German Writings*, AE 34:285–86.
4   *Preface to Luther's German Writings*, AE 34:286.

how sweet, how lovely, how mighty, how comforting God's Word is, wisdom beyond all wisdom. . . . For as soon as God's Word takes root and grows in you, the devil will harry you, and will make a real doctor of you, and by his assaults will teach you to seek and love God's Word.[5]

ABOUT THOSE TRIALS

Amen and Amen! If we did not have trials, we wouldn't pray much and wouldn't seek out God's Word much. But the trials pull everything together and drive us into Christ's blessed life, death, resurrection, and life eternal.

Trials always come. They tempt us to believe that the Gospel is not ours, that Scripture is not true, that God does not really love us, that He might even hate us and want to punish us, if He exists at all. The art of being a Christian is, in large measure, believing in the God of promise against the God of trial. We believe the clear Word of the Gospel: free forgiveness and trust in Baptism, Absolution, and Christ's body and blood in the Supper for forgiveness. We trust His promises against the pain, death, spiritual struggles, and disappointments we have in this life and which God allows and even brings upon us. Does God will suffering? Contemplate Jesus' prayer in the garden for the answer: "Father, if You are willing, remove this cup from Me. Nevertheless, not My will, but Yours, be done" (Luke 22:42). To be a Christian is to experience suffering, yet to trust that it is sent for good, not harm. It is to pray with Job: "Though [God] slay me, I will hope in Him" (Job 13:15).

TENTATIO, MEDITATIO, ORATIO: TRIAL, MEDITATION, PRAYER

Open on my kneeler is the *Lutheran Service Book Altar Book*, which contains all the Psalms. The Psalms are God's prayer book for us. Jesus had them memorized. They express the full range of human emotion—frustration, pain, faithlessness, but also happiness,

---

5   *Preface to Luther's German Writings*, AE 34:286–87.

joy, and steadfastness. They tell us who God is and how He regards us. They have their own contexts, such as prayers for royal events. But they console us now because they tell us that God acted in the past, He promises to act today, and He shall continue to act for the well-being of His saints into the future (Psalm 145). The enemies of the faithful remain the same: the devil, the world, and our flesh. The weaknesses of Christians are the same: doubt, sin, and faithlessness.

My trials have driven me to the Psalms. I am daily shocked and delighted at how the words I pray from 3,000 years ago are so applicable now. I am struck low by the Law and raised to life by the Gospel. "I said, 'I will confess my transgressions to the LORD,' and You forgave the iniquity of my sin" (Psalm 32:5; see Psalm 130; 143). I resonate with the complaints of David (Psalm 9; 10; 124; 129). I am led to give thanks to God for His manifold blessings to the contrite (Psalm 147). Time and time again, the inspired and living words of these prayers pray me into joy and rejoicing. "Be glad in the LORD, and rejoice, O righteous, and shout for joy, all you upright in heart!" (Psalm 32:11; see Psalm 122; 126). I am consoled by the Lord's promises (Psalm 119:151).

More than any other prayers, the Psalms lead us directly to the life St. Paul wills for us because it is Christ's will for us: "Rejoice always, pray without ceasing, give thanks in all circumstances; for this is the will of God in Christ Jesus for you" (1 Thessalonians 5:16–18). As Luther observed, trials drive us to rely on God's Word, and they drive us into prayer.

In my feeble walk of faith, in my challenged prayer life, through a multitude of trials, the Psalms have been a solace. Raising children and grandchildren; facing illness, tragedy, or problems in the family or at work; struggling with faith because of assaults of the sinful flesh and the devil—all of this drives us to prayer and meditation on God's Word. That's how God makes "theologians" or "Christians" of us. That's what He did with the prophets (Genesis 22). That's what He did with the apostles (2 Corinthians 12). That's what He does with you.

Why Do I Believe
in Jesus?

....

J esus grabbed me by the neck in 1962 at a font in little old
Bethel Lutheran Church in the Iowa farming town of Lawton.
I have no recollection of a time when I did not know that Jesus
was my Savior. I often think that I grew up at the "end of sanity."
There wasn't much crime to speak of. No drugs really. I walked
to and from school from kindergarten on with no worries of
abduction or sexual predators. Culture and church, Boy Scouts,
school—widely supported by a shared morality and favorable
view of Christianity. But things change.

Today's world is a postmodern cultural collage. That's not all bad!
Prior to the fall of the Berlin Wall, teetering modernism was in its
last gasp, asserting that this or that philosophical or political theory
could encompass all truth. Would science unlock the mysteries of
life and the universe? People believed the answer was "Yes!" The
modernists discounted the spiritual realm, opting for psychological
theories to explain the human experience. They all grasped for truth
and found parts of it, but the complexities of the human individual,
the collective community, simply evaded encapsulation. And every
new discovery, whether at the atomic level or about the universe, has
unfolded complexity upon complexity. The most shocking thing is the
repeated discovery of order—ordered genetic information in biology
and complex order in the universe. It was famously asserted that the
probability of life coming about randomly would be about the same
odds as a tornado sweeping through a junkyard and assembling a
747, fully fueled and ready for takeoff. Atheism requires too much
faith for me.

The question I had to grapple with—the question everyone has to deal with—is "What do you make of Jesus?" Most people will respond with morality. Jesus was a great man who left the world great ethics, like "Love your neighbor as yourself." But Jesus' ethics can all be found in other religions. What makes Jesus unique is His claim to be the divine Son of God who came to give His life as a ransom (Mark 10:45).

And did He or did He not rise from the dead? The resurrection accounts of the Bible have all the sober signs of reality. Their complex details are told from different viewpoints, which are not easily harmonized. I also find it compelling that there are no records of squabbles among Jesus' living followers over what actually took place. Others discounted or contested the facts, but they were either contemporary opponents of Jesus or came much later, after Jesus' immediate followers were all dead. And finally, Jesus' apostles preached the death and resurrection of Jesus and suffered all, even death, to do so. They believed it happened.

I believe it too, because "faith comes from hearing, and hearing through the word of Christ" (Romans 10:17). Jesus has grabbed my black heart with forgiveness. My reason follows after, in the wake of faith, and convinces me that the universe is simply too ordered and too complex to exist by chance. And the only way that the life of Jesus makes any sense is if what the Bible says about Him actually happened.

Why does anyone believe in Jesus? Certainly because the Holy Spirit has called a person by the Gospel. But the explanations that resonate with any individual's reason and senses are good gifts also. It's kind of like a marriage: a woman is a man's wife because their marriage certificate says so. But all the things she loves about him are what make that certificate more than a bare fact of history, and they animate their marriage with purpose and joy. The question of why one believes in Jesus is worth asking, investigating, and supporting with study and prayer. The reasons for the hope we have are testimonies to the divine blessings of the human mind and heart. So, why do you believe in Jesus?

Visitation Encouragement

....

Mary was visited by the angel Gabriel. "Behold, you will conceive in your womb and bear a son, and you shall call His name Jesus" (Luke 1:31).

Mary visited Elizabeth, who was also with child (John the Baptizer), and John leapt for joy in the womb! (Luke 1:41).

Jesus was born at Bethlehem for the great divine visitation of God in the flesh!

Jesus' first visit to the temple brought consolation and joy to old Simeon: "Lord, now You are letting Your servant depart in peace" (Luke 2:29).

Jesus visited the temple at age 12 so that He might teach then and teach us today: "Did you not know that I must be in My Father's house?" (Luke 2:49).

And Jesus' visitation continued throughout His life. He went to Nazareth and preached, "Today this Scripture has been fulfilled in your hearing" (Luke 4:21). He visited Capernaum and healed a man with a demon (Luke 4:35). He went to Peter's house and healed his mother-in-law, as well as many others (Luke 4:38–39). Jesus was on the move along the Lake of Gennesaret when He began calling His apostles (Luke 5:1–11). Jesus moved about cleansing lepers, healing paralytics, and calling an apostle named Matthew. All the way to the cross, Jesus is on the move, visiting this and that place, teaching, consoling, rebuking, and encouraging! When He appeared to His disciples after the resurrection, He bade them baptize and teach as they were on the move ("Going, therefore . . . ," Matthew 28:19, author's translation).

Prior to the Reformation, bishops weren't doing much. Some simply held the title for the sake of the property and money associated with the office, and they paid others to do the work. Luther, in his Church Order for Wittenberg (1528), noted that visitation is what bishops ("overseers") are to do, just as we see Jesus, the Old Testament prophets, and Sts. Paul and Barnabas going about. They go "not for a nice walk" (Luther), but they are constantly visiting to extend the Gospel, to encourage, to speak the Law, and to forgive and console (Acts 15:30–41).

The Bible and the Lutheran Confessions teach that all pastors are "bishops" or ecclesiastical "overseers." ("Bishop" is a translation of the Greek word "overseer.") Visitation is the sacred duty of every pastor or "bishop." The ministry of Jesus, the apostles, and St. Paul was translocal—that is, it was not tied to any one place. But even though a pastor has a local call, he is the visitor of that place. The ministry is peripatetic (the Greek word for "walking around")! A pastor visits the neighborhood to share the Gospel of Christ. He seeks the lost, just like Jesus (Luke 19:10). He goes to find the lost sheep. He visits the faithful, rejoicing with them when they rejoice, and consoling them and mourning with them when they are sad. His energy to circulate the Word helps locate his congregation at the heart of the community where the Lord has situated them, where every person needs to be washed in the blood of Jesus.

The office of "bishop" (in the sense of an overseer of other pastors) arose in the early centuries of the church. It is not mandated in the Bible, nor is it of the essence of the church, but it is for the well-being of the church. Our LCMS fathers understood this very well, as did Luther. The heart of this office is visitation. That's why visitation figures so intensely in the constitution of the LCMS, especially with respect to the offices of president, district president, and circuit visitor. A healthy congregation has a visiting pastor. A healthy district has a visiting district president. A healthy circuit has a visiting circuit visitor.

It's not easy, to be sure, but this is the way we maintain doctrinal unity in the truth of the Holy Scriptures, which is confessed in the Book of Concord. Visitation is how we care for one another. It is how we serve one another. It is how we hold one another accountable to the offices and duties we bear for the sake of the church. It is how we speak a word of Law, if needed. ("Hey, pastor, you're kinda neglecting your wife and family . . ." "Hey, congregation, you have a habit of beating up on your church workers. It must stop.") Oh, how our church workers and struggling congregations need encouragement!

If you want explicit and helpful examples of visitation, read of Jesus trekking about Palestine and what He does as He moves. Read Paul's letters. He preaches the Gospel. He speaks the Law as needed. He confronts unbelievers with the resurrected Christ. He consoles. He seeks consolation for himself. He encourages. He sets things in order. He sends people to do what needs to be done in different places. He responds to questions about difficult situations in congregations. He's much more patient than I would be! "O foolish Galatians!" (Galatians 3:1).

While we speak of "visitation" as the work of pastors and church officials, every layperson also does well to be busy in his or her many vocations, actively encouraging and sharing Christ, loving his or her family and those nearby at work and home. Luther said that all our needs were met by Christ visiting us and taking on our flesh as a babe at Bethlehem. He also said that our neighbor's need is our vocation to mercy. And he called faith a "busy, active, meddlesome thing"![1] God grant us all the loving initiative to visit our neighbors for the sake of the Gospel.

---

1   See *Preface to the Epistle to the Romans*, AE 35:370.

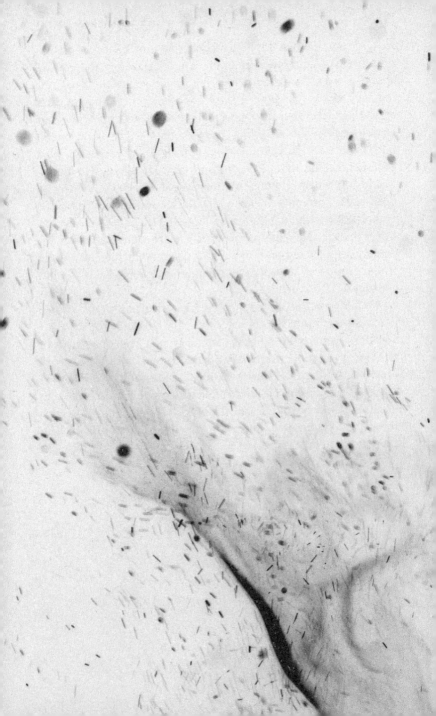

PART II

Courage to Confess

. . . .

Lutherans are confessing people. More than any other Christian tradition, we define ourselves by a set of formal confessions that were born out of intense erudition and profound reverence for the holy Word of God.

Confession shapes the Lutheran mind so deeply that we might not even recognize how uniquely skilled we are for the task. The way we think and the prayer we breathe reveals the Lutheran commitment to proclaim God's Word faithfully.

Our neighbors are increasingly deprived of protections society once provided by law and custom. The message of Law and Gospel is an unparalleled gift the Lord has given us to share with scared, hurting people by our own words and acts. With God's help, each of our lives may be "a high doxology Unto the holy Trinity" (*Lutheran Worship* 319:4).

Encourage
One Another

. . . .

Paul says it twice: "Encourage one another." Both times, he is concluding his argument about the imminent day of Jesus' return and the comfort that gives Christians. The first time, he begins by dealing with the dead.

> But we do not want you to be uninformed, brothers, about those who are asleep, that you may not grieve as others do who have no hope. For since we believe that Jesus died and rose again, even so, through Jesus, God will bring with Him those who have fallen asleep. For this we declare to you by a word from the Lord, that we who are alive, who are left until the coming of the Lord, will not precede those who have fallen asleep. For the Lord Himself will descend from heaven with a cry of command, with the voice of an archangel, and with the sound of the trumpet of God. And the dead in Christ will rise first. Then we who are alive, who are left, will be caught up together with them in the clouds to meet the Lord in the air, and so we will always be with the Lord. *Therefore encourage one another with these words.* (1 Thessalonians 4:13–18, emphasis added)

Don't let the death of loved ones discourage you, Paul argues. Although they have gone before you into death, we will all be together with the Lord Jesus at the resurrection. *Therefore, encourage one another* with these words.

Let the resurrection encourage you in the face of the death of loved ones. Let the sure and certain Word of God be the instrument by which you encourage one another, build one another up, call one another together.

Just a few verses later in the epistle, Paul again concludes with a command for the Thessalonian Christians to encourage one another. Again, he begins by stressing how soon the day of Jesus' return is.

> **Now concerning the times and the seasons, brothers, you have no need to have anything written to you. For you yourselves are fully aware that the day of the Lord will come like a thief in the night. While people are saying, "There is peace and security," then sudden destruction will come upon them as labor pains come upon a pregnant woman, and they will not escape. But you are not in darkness, brothers, for that day to surprise you like a thief. . . . For God has not destined us for wrath, but to obtain salvation through our Lord Jesus Christ, who died for us so that whether we are awake or asleep we might live with Him.** *Therefore encourage one another and build one another up,* **just as you are doing.** (1 Thessalonians 5:1–4, 9–11, emphasis added)

Encouraging one another to remember that Jesus will return to us is a churchly work we can be bold and happy to take up. It always does your neighbor good to hear this message, and it always does you good to confess it.

Courage to Confess

··

There is a fabulous Greek word, *homologeo*, which means to "say the same thing." In the New Testament it is often translated as "confession" and encompasses three important aspects of the Christian faith:

1. *The confession of sins.* "If we *confess* our sins, [God] is faithful and just to forgive us our sins and to cleanse us from all unrighteousness" (1 John 1:9).

2. *The confession of the content of the faith.* "Whoever *confesses Me* before men, him I will also confess before My Father who is in heaven" (Matthew 10:32 NKJV). This means to confess Jesus to be the Son of God, Savior of the world.

3. The confession of praise. "I *confess* [usually translated as "praise" or "thank," but the root of the word is the same as "confess"] You, Father . . ." (Matthew 11:25).

All three shades of meaning belong together.

If the strong confession of sin is missing, there is no real understanding of our urgent need for a Savior. Luther said that if a "mere man" were in the scale over against our sins, and not the divine-human Son of God, we'd be lost. That's a strong confession of who Jesus is. If we confess our sins, but have no idea of the divine remedy for our sins in the doctrine of Christ—in justification and atonement (Romans 3–4), reconciliation (2 Corinthians 5:19), Holy Baptism (1 Peter 3:21), Holy Absolution (John 20:21–23), the Lord's Supper (1 Corinthians 11:23–26), etc.—then we'd be in bad shape, prone to look for human remedies for sin. What wretches we are, indeed, if the recognition of our sin, of who Christ is for us, and of all He's done for us doesn't cause us to well up in praise and thanksgiving and, yes, joy (Philippians 4:4)!

From the beginning, Christ called forth a confession. "But who do you say that I am?" Jesus asked His disciples (Matthew 16:15). From the beginning, there were departures from God's Word that required a confession of the true faith.

The "ecumenical creeds"—the Apostles', Nicene, and Athanasian Creeds—were the Church's response to any rejection of the Bible's teaching. (Luther at one point throws in the Te Deum for good measure as a confession of praise!)

At the time of the Lutheran Reformation, a clear confession was required again. Our Lutheran Book of Concord is that confession. Salvation, according to the Bible, is a free act of divine grace. Salvation was achieved by Christ's cross and resurrection and is delivered by the Word of the Gospel and by the Sacraments. Faith alone lays hold of the gift. Christ alone is the way to salvation. The Bible alone is the source of all divine truth.

Lutherans assert that it does not suffice to say simply "my confession is the Bible." There's hardly a religion in the sphere of Christianity that doesn't claim to confess the Bible. Even the most esoteric and non-Christian religions claim to use the Bible! (For example, Jehovah's Witnesses deny the Trinity and the divinity of Christ.) But Lutherans confess the Bible as it is rightly understood: *the Bible is its own interpreter.* We use reason, logic, and grammar as servants, not as masters of the biblical text. The Lutheran Confessions rightly set forth the teaching of the Scriptures. The Bible is God's Word and is normative for us. The Lutheran Confessions (known most popularly in Luther's catechisms) are a secondary authority that derive their authority from the Scriptures. By requiring public allegiance to the Book of Concord, all our congregations, church workers, and institutions together confess: "Yes, this Book of Concord is a true confession of the teachings of the Bible. Because this is so, these confessions are normative for us."

Church historian Hermann Sasse loved to point out that those who de-emphasized or ignored our public confession in the Book of

Concord soon gave up the authority of the Bible too! The Lutheran Confessions are a great benefit in countless ways:

- They focus us on the Gospel of Jesus.
- They teach us that the messages of the Law and the Gospel are always relevant.
- They free us from human attempts to obtain divine merit by directing us to Christ alone.
- They clearly condemn false teachings that have arisen in the Church.
- They instruct us that the Lutheran Church is the catholic church gone right.
- They teach us that there is salvation also outside the orthodox Lutheran Church, for there is salvation wherever Christ is known and believed.
- The Book of Concord teaches that Lutherans are conservative, retaining worship and ceremonies so long as they don't contradict the Gospel.
- It teaches that there is great freedom in matters of worship, but that such matters should be in the service of the Gospel, with great care to avoid offense.
- The Lutheran Confessions teach that Christ came for all people and that the Lutheran Church as the church of the pure Gospel of grace in Christ is therefore a church about mission until Jesus returns.

I like to think of the Book of Concord as a beautiful pasture with hills, valleys, and streams. It provides an untold number of places to graze for teaching, edification, consolation, comfort, surety, direction for living in Christ, and more. But the pasture has a fence. Within the pasture, I may graze freely. I may freely think and come to fresh understandings of the biblical texts and teaching of the Church. But I do not step outside the fence, lest I fall into false teaching that threatens the Gospel. That strong fence is also a protection for the grazing sheep. No congregation, no institution, no church worker, and especially no pastor should presume to live and work within the confines of the pasture if they knowingly reject the biblical teachings of our Lutheran Confessions. To do so is disingenuous.

In recent years, Concordia Publishing House has sold well over 100,000 copies of *Concordia: The Lutheran Confessions—A Reader's Edition of the Book of Concord*. Get a copy if you don't have one already! You'll find a wealth of helpful material in addition to the confessions of the Lutheran Church. And you'll find that your comprehension of the depth of our need and the greatness of Christ and His gifts will deepen, broaden, and embolden your joyous praise of God, Father, Son, and Holy Spirit.

How Luther
Became Lutheran

··

Luther's Reformation insights did not come in one fell swoop on October 31, 1517. Far from it. He'd been lecturing on the Bible at the University of Wittenberg for several years, teaching courses on Romans and the Psalms. He'd come to a clear conviction that humility was key to the Christian life—that is, the recognition of one's sinfulness in the sight of a holy God. Already in 1516 he could write to a struggling friend: "Christ dwells only in sinners."[1] But this line of thought had existed before in medieval theology.

The indulgence controversy pushed Luther forward and into Scripture. Thesis 1 of the *Ninety-Five Theses* states: "When our Lord and Master Jesus Christ said, 'Repent,' he willed the entire life of believers to be one of repentance."[2] Luther had come to see that "repentance" and the Roman Catholic practice of "penance" to pay for the alleged temporal punishments for sin were not the same thing. The Roman Church had taught that purgatory had to be suffered for thousands of years to pay off temporal punishments for sins. Indulgences were dreamed up to shorten the time in purgatory. Indulgences could be gotten by viewing relics of this or that saint. (The Wittenberg Castle Church was full of them.) Or they could be obtained by paying cold, hard cash.

This caused Luther to blow his pastoral stack, as it were. Even at this early point, it agonized him to have people claiming to be Christians and then living like swine without consequence because they had a piece of paper with a papal seal granting full remission

---

1   Letter to George Spenlein, AE 48:13.
2   *Ninety-Five Theses*, AE 31:25.

of all sins—past, present, and future. Tetzel the indulgence pusher preached that these papers would get a person into heaven "even if he had . . . violated the mother of God"![3]

Luther hit the church where it lived. He threatened its finances. The indulgences were being sold to finance a Prussian royal family's acquisition of an episcopal seat. Albert of Mainz became cardinal archbishop by paying the pope a large sum for the position. To do that, he had to borrow millions from the Fuggers, a banking family in Augsburg. Albert then hired Johann Tetzel as the fund developer to raise money to pay back the loan. Pope Leo X was happy to receive those payments so he could continue construction of St. Peter's in Rome, including employing expensive artists such as Michaelangelo. (A famous Roman Catholic historian once described Leo X as having not the slightest pastoral interest in his entire being.)

The authorities came down on this little monk in obscure Wittenberg. Luther was driven further into the Scriptures. In the months after posting his theses, he was lecturing on the Letter to the Hebrews. He came to see the nature and significance of Christ's once-for-all sacrifice on the cross. He lectured also on Paul's Letter to the Galatians.

Luther scholar Martin Brecht suggests that Luther's reformatory breakthrough occurred sometime after the nailing of his *Ninety-Five Theses* to the church door. By February 1518, Luther was convinced that true Christian righteousness meant that the Christian despaired of his own righteousness. Then, in a sermon on Philippians 2:5–6 delivered possibly on Palm Sunday in 1519, Luther preached on "two kinds of righteousness." Here Luther fully describes the Christian's righteousness as Christ's righteousness. The Christian's relationship to Christ is like a marriage. Christ gets my sin, death, hell, punishment, etc. I get Christ's birth, life, sinlessness, suffering, death, resurrection and eternal life! Luther called it the "happy exchange."[4]

And happy it is, indeed! "He made Him to be sin who knew no sin, so that in Him we might become the righteousness of God"

---

3   *Ninety-Five Theses*, Thesis 75, AE 31:32.
4   See *Freedom of a Christian*, AE 31:351–52.

(2 Corinthians 5:21). Simple as that. Profound. But muddled in the church for a thousand years before Luther. And it's still muddled today.

This doctrine of the justification of the sinner before God for Christ's sake, by grace, received by faith alone, is the gift given to Luther for the whole church. The Lutheran Church today still has the honor and task to teach and preach it far and wide with Luther's compassion-driven fervor. We shall do so until our last breath, for the salvation of souls. God grant it.

Let's Be
Who We Are

The first step in being better than you are is to be who you are.

The LCMS is a large and complex organization, but congregations are the fundamental and divinely mandated building block of the Synod. The Church is Christians gathered about the rightly preached Word of God and the properly administered Sacraments. That's why we have pastors. Christians bear witness to Christ wherever they live and work. Not much beyond that is mandated by the Bible. There are manifold viewpoints on different issues and challenges the Church faces. The Bible grants great freedom for congregations to respond to the needs and mission opportunities that confront them in their various contexts.

Together, however, we do have a strong and clear confession of the faith. Every church worker and congregation pledges to uphold and be subject to the truth of Holy Scripture as God's divine and inerrant Word and to confess the Lutheran Confessions as a true exposition of Holy Scripture.

The Synod went wobbly on the inspiration and inerrancy of the Bible from the late 1950s into the 1970s. A host of issues began to be viewed by some as undecided and open questions—a six-day creation, the existence of Adam and Eve, prophecies of Christ in the Old Testament, the historical truth of the Bible, the virgin birth of Christ, the nature of His resurrection, the presence of Christ's body and blood in the Sacrament, church fellowship, closed Communion, the church's mission work, and more. These views were quite "new" to the Synod and at odds with what had been confessed from its beginning in 1847. The more these views were spread around the Synod, the more disruption, disagreement, antagonism, and, worst of all, political rancor took hold.

After the Synod reasserted its confession (e.g., *A Statement of Scriptural and Confessional Principles*), it was not but a decade before a new challenge arose in the so-called "church growth movement." Beginning in the 1980s, debates swirled about contemporary worship, the liturgy, the role of the pastor, the role of the laity, and so on. Then came a decision to allow men to serve as pastors long term, without actually being made pastors via call and ordination. That brought division and controversy. We have learned through the process of making these men pastors that many of them suffered from bad consciences for serving as pastors without a call and ordination.

WHO ARE WE?

The first step in being better than you are is to be who you are. Every day that I wake up as Synod president, I resolve to do what's right. When I was called to be head of LCMS World Relief and Human Care, I met with Dr. Alvin Barry to get his advice. (Little did I know that he would die just a few weeks later.) His advice to me was very simple: "Every day, walk across the road and pick up a stone and carry it to the other side. Pretty soon, you'll notice that you've moved quite a pile." He gave me that advice not 10 feet from where I'm writing right now. Folksy, but true.

The LCMS has plenty of warts and imperfections. That's always true of the Church on this earth (see Paul's letters to Galatia and Corinth). But she's the best thing going. When I say we ought to be who we are, I'm not saying that we shouldn't innovate, think outside the box, try something new, take a risk for the sake of the Gospel mission. I'm saying, in all these things we cannot and must not lose our fundamental, biblical, and confessional bearings, defined as they are by the Gospel.

- *Let's be who we are.* "The Son of Man came to seek and to save the lost" (Luke 19:10). "Go therefore and make disciples of all nations" (Matthew 28:19). "But you are a chosen race, a royal priesthood, a holy nation, a people for His own possession, that you may proclaim the excellencies of Him who called you out of darkness into His marvelous light" (1 Peter 2:9).

- *Let's be who we are.* "All Scripture is breathed out by God" (2 Timothy 3:16).

- *Let's be who we are.* "By grace you are saved through faith, and that not of yourselves; it is the gift of God" (Ephesians 2:8 NKJV).

- *Let's be who we are.* "Baptism . . . now saves you" (1 Peter 3:21).

- *Let's be who we are.* "If you forgive the sins of any, they are forgiven them" (John 20:23).

- *Let's be who we are.* "Drink of it, all of you, for this is My blood of the covenant, which is poured out for many for the forgiveness of sins" (Matthew 26:27).

- *Let's be who we are*, "rightly handling the word of truth" (2 Timothy 2:15). We are the Lutheran Church, the church of Law and Gospel. We are the Missouri Synod, whose first president wrote the greatest book ever on Law and Gospel!

- *Let's be who we are.* As the Synod in convention has asserted many times (84 percent at the 2016 convention), there is plenty of room for flexibility in worship, but we don't ditch Confession and Absolution. We don't ditch the Scripture readings. We don't ditch the Creed. We don't ditch faithful Law and Gospel preaching. We don't mess with the Lord's Words of Institution. Doing so amounts to ditching the Gospel!

- *Let's be who we are.* As Hermann Sasse pointed out, the LCMS is unique in both highly treasuring the office of pastor ("Let them do this with joy and not with groaning, for that would be of no advantage to you," Hebrews 13:17) and having a faithful, active laity, deeply involved in the life and mission of the Church.

- *Let's be who we are.* God treasures children, families, and education. So do we.

- *Let's be who we are.* Pastors are "servants of Christ and stewards of the mysteries of God" (1 Corinthians 4:1; see also the Apology of the Augsburg Confession XXIV 78–80). There is pastoral discretion in giving the Lord's Supper, and we grant it, but simply placing a notice in the bulletin inviting non-LCMS people to the Sacrament without any contact with the pastor is not pastoral discretion. And by the way, the LCMS has a higher retention of members than churches practicing open Communion. Let's be who we say we are.

The office you have placed me in has many responsibilities. The one repeated most often in the LCMS constitution and bylaws is that of doing whatever the president can to uphold the public teaching, doctrine, and practice of the LCMS. That includes fervent desire to reach out with the Gospel. Until my last hour in this office, I will press toward this goal. God help us all. And He does.

Only Jesus

....

And there is salvation in no one else, for there is no other name under heaven given among men by which we must be saved. (Acts 4:12)

Celebrating 175 years is important. But it's a brief period compared to the 500th anniversary of the Lutheran Reformation. It's less significant still compared to the 2,000-year history of the Lord's Church, and it pales in comparison to the 4,000 years since the call of Abraham and the promise of the Savior given to him by the Lord.

In the past decade of serving the congregations of the Synod, I've learned that I am not that significant either, especially in the history of the Synod. God works what He wills despite our insignificance. If a new Lutheran church body began today with fourteen congregations, it would be the butt of unending jokes, as was the Missouri Synod in 1847. If it were to claim that its constitution was the restoration of the authority of the inerrant Scriptures, the Lutheran Confessions, and authentic New Testament Christianity, it would be ignored, laughed at, and scorned. If it claimed the Bible and Luther's catechism are absolutely true, that there is no other God than the Holy Trinity, and no salvation outside of faith in Christ and His blessed cross and resurrection, its founders would be accosted as kooks by contemporaries.

How insignificant were fourteen congregations and a handful of pastors 175 years ago? They knew they were numerically insignificant. They knew they were the object of ridicule in a world awash in agnosticism, especially in the church. They lamented the state of their mother churches in Europe where the Gospel had largely been supplanted by mere morality. Even pastors no longer believed the Word of God.

Like ours, their world was in chaos. Revolutions shook all of Europe in 1848. Atheism was rife among German immigrants to North America. A cholera epidemic raged in the United States in 1849 and killed thousands. The liberal Germans in St. Louis attacked the Saxons from the moment they stepped off the boat. The LCMS was poor, small, and weak, and they knew it. They were far-flung, from Michigan, Indiana, Ohio, Buffalo, and St. Louis, so they were lonely. But they were certain of one thing: Luther's Reformation had rediscovered and reasserted the truth of the free forgiveness of sins in the blessed Gospel of Christ, delivered by the Word, distributed in Baptism and in Christ's body and blood in the Sacrament. They came from various backgrounds. Some had been theological liberals (including Wilhelm Sihler). Many had been pietists (overemphasizing religious feelings as the ground of faith and certainty over the objective teachings of the Bible and catechism). Personal crises had driven a number of them to believe the Bible, read the Lutheran Confessions, and confess the old teachings of the Lutheran Church as the teachings of Scripture.

Through Dr. C. F. W. Walther's newspaper, *The Lutheran* (*Der Lutheraner*), they discovered one another. They corresponded. They hatched a plan for a Lutheran synod (*synod* means "together on the same road" in Greek), crafted a constitution (which still survives, mostly word for word in the present LCMS constitution), and officially brought the church body into existence in Chicago on April 26, 1847. The Missouri Saxons brought their log cabin seminary after Wilhelm Loehe gave the Synod a seminary in Fort Wayne, Indiana. They embarked on a mission to share the Gospel far and wide and were keenly aware of their divine mandate to "seek and save the lost." They educated pastors and sent them to shepherd the thousands upon thousands of German-speaking immigrants spreading across the wide reaches of North America. They planted churches for Germans who had left their homeland for economic promise and had come from weak churches in the old country. In New York and Boston, they met the immigrants as they came off the boats and sent them across the fruited plain to German communities served by pastors. Walther and others spoke English, but they concentrated on German-speaking communities because of the enormous opportunity and volume of work. Eventually, they were only too happy to help found an "English Synod," which became the "English District" of the LCMS (1911).

Just like 175 years ago, war has returned to Europe. We've suffered a global pandemic. The church is in grave decline in the West. Just google "decline of the church in the West" for shocking statistics, particularly in the United States. The "woke" culture ubiquitous on university campuses around the world has created a culture of sexual ambiguity. In some ways, the LCMS is doing slightly better than many churches, but we, too, are heavily affected. Easy fixes are mythical. Our children are bombarded from the earliest age with the lies of a morally adrift culture. For sixty years, the sexual revolution has taught that sex is a subjective, personal choice, and that one may be one's own creator. Our governments support "sex change" operations even for minors. The abortion of a child as an inconvenient by-product at odds with one's own self-determination is one of the greatest indicators of the denial of our Creator and His will for His creatures, created male and female. (For more on this, read Carl Trueman, *The Rise and Triumph of the Modern Self* [Wheaton, IL: Crossway, 2020].) Apocalyptic times indeed. Come, Lord Jesus!

What's the answer? What's our task? What's our message? Only Jesus. "There is no other name under heaven given among men by which we must be saved" (Acts 4:12).

Today, we are just under 6,000 congregations. Is our constitution antiquated? Not unless the Word of God is antiquated: "The word of the Lord remains forever" (1 Peter 1:25). Today, we have 5,700 active pastors sharing Christ, day in and day out. We have the largest Protestant parochial school system in the United States. We have thousands of teachers sharing the message with "the least of these." *Your Creator is the triune God. He has made you. You are His. Only Jesus is your Savior. And He has redeemed you as His very own creature.*

We equip our people with Jesus; fortify our mothers and fathers; strengthen homes to love, teach, and prepare children for life in this world with its challenges and blessings; shore up our men to be men of God and defend places where our women can be women of Christ.

Today, we face the hatred and ridicule of the world, a world in chaos. Our fathers and mothers in the faith faced the same. Today, we face the same threat of loneliness and isolation they did. Whether the loneliest pastor and tiniest congregation in the farthest reaches of the earth or the president of the Synod, we are terribly insignificant. Imagine those fourteen lonely congregations in 1847. What a difference it made for them to be joined in faith and love in the Lutheran confession.

Today, we face very similar challenges. The decline of Christianity in the West presents us with the greatest challenge in the modern history of the church. With Jesus, and only Jesus, we shall go forth nevertheless: "Go therefore and make disciples of all nations, baptizing them in the name of the Father and of the Son and of the Holy Spirit, teaching them to observe all that I have commanded you. And behold, I am with you always, to the end of the age" (Matthew 28:19–20). "Let us hold fast the confession of our hope without wavering, for He who promised is faithful" (Hebrews 10:23).

Who we are—a 175-year-old church body—is important, even though it pales in comparison to the history of the church. But what we do—preaching and pointing to Jesus for 175 years—is significant indeed. It has eternal consequences. If 175 years is an accomplishment, it's Christ's accomplishment. Come what may, the next 175 years are in the hands of Jesus, only Jesus, and so are we.

175 Years
of Only Jesus

. . . .

And there is salvation in no one else, for there is no other name under heaven given among men by which we must be saved. (Acts 4:12)

Only Jesus.

Planned from eternity, prophesied of old, the offspring of the woman "shall [crush his] head" (Genesis 3:15). "The stone that the builders rejected has become the cornerstone" (Psalm 118:22). "The Word became flesh and dwelt among us" (John 1:14). Only Jesus.

"Born of woman, born under the law" (Galatians 4:4). Like every person in the history of the planet, yet without sin (see Hebrews 4:15). "For our sake He made Him to be sin who knew no sin, so that in Him we might become the righteousness of God" (2 Corinthians 5:21). Only Jesus.

"You shall call His name Jesus, for He will save His people from their sins" (Matthew 1:21). Yeshua. Joshua. Yahweh saves! "No one comes to the Father except through Me" (John 14:6). Only Jesus!

Solomon said, "Look to the temple, for the Lord Yahweh dwells there with His name for forgiveness." Now we proclaim: "Let the whole world bow and confess that Jesus is Lord, to the glory of God the Father!" (see Philippians 2:5–11). The name is Jesus. Only Jesus.

Look to the whole of the Old Testament. Read the Law. Read the prophets. Read the Psalms. The punishment that brought us peace was upon Him; "with His wounds we are healed" (Isaiah 53:5). Jesus said, "[These Scriptures are] they that bear witness about Me" (John 5:39). Only Jesus!

"Don't speak in that name," the authorities told the apostles (see Acts 4:18). Speak of gods aplenty. Speak of Caesar god. Only not that name Jesus. Only *not* Jesus.

But there's a compulsion. "The Son of Man is going to be delivered into . . ." (Mark 9:31). "The Son of Man must suffer many things . . . and be killed" (Luke 9:22). "The Scriptures must be fulfilled" (Mark 14:49 NIV). "Sir, we wish to see Jesus," the Greeks said to Philip (John 12:21). Right away Jesus says, "Unless a grain of wheat falls into the earth and dies, it remains alone; but if it dies, it bears much fruit" (John 12:24). The Son of Man must be glorified. Crucified. Raised. It has to be . . . only Jesus.

The apostles have forever borne witness. That "which we have heard, which we have seen with our eyes, which we looked upon and have touched with our hands . . . we proclaim also to you, so that you too may have fellowship with us," and have joy and life eternal (1 John 1:1–4). Only Jesus.

"No other name . . . by which we must be saved" (Acts 4:12). Tell us not to, ridicule us, slander us, beat us, imprison us, pass laws against Jesus, do what you will—we *must* speak of what we have seen and heard. Only Jesus.

What is Baptism? Our doing? No. The apostle says it's Jesus. It is being clothed with His righteousness, connected to His death and resurrection. Only Jesus.

What is preaching? It's the Gospel. It's forgiveness. "I tell you your sins are forgiven." It's about living forgiven. Only Jesus.

What's the Supper? It's Jesus! It's all Jesus. His body. His blood. Given and shed. Take and eat, for forgiveness. Only Jesus.

The Judaizers gave St. Paul fits. It's not *only* Jesus, they said. It's Jesus plus circumcision; it's Jesus plus the law which equals salvation. The apostolic council—referenced over and over in the literature of the founding of the LCMS—replied, "We're not putting the yoke of the ceremonial law upon new believers." Only Jesus.

The medieval church went off the rails. Baptism and merit. Absolution and satisfaction/merit. Supper and merit. Priesthood and merit. Serve and *maybe* be saved. Jesus and merit. Luther read: "[The

Gospel] is the power of God for salvation . . . from faith for faith" (Romans 1:16–17). And Jesus grabbed him. Jesus said, "[I] came not to be served but to serve, and to give [My] life as a ransom for many" (Mark 10:45). That turned the entire trajectory of the church. Jesus does the verbs for salvation, redemption, sanctification. All Jesus. Ever Jesus. Only Jesus.

There's a wonderful section of Luther's Smalcald Articles—and because we're in the Missouri Synod, we have to read a passage from the Confessions in a 175th anniversary sermon. Listen to this:

> The first and chief article is this:
>
> Jesus Christ, our God and Lord, died for our sins and was raised for our justification (Romans 4:24–25).
>
> He alone is the Lamb of God who takes away the sins of the world (John 1:29), and God has laid upon Him the iniquities of us all (Isaiah 53:6).
>
> All have sinned and are justified freely, without their own works or merits, by His grace, through the redemption that is in Christ Jesus, in His blood (Romans 3:23–25).
>
> This is necessary to believe. This cannot be otherwise acquired or grasped by any work, law, or merit. Therefore, it is clear and certain that this faith alone justifies us. As St. Paul says:
>
>> For we hold that one is justified by faith apart from works of the law. (Romans 3:28)
>>
>> That He might be just and the justifier of the one who has faith in Jesus. [Romans 3:26]
>
> Nothing of this article can be yielded or surrendered, even though heaven and earth and everything else falls [Mark 13:31].
>
>> For there is no other name under heaven given among men by which we must be saved. (Acts 4:12) (Smalcald Articles II I 1–5)

The early fathers and mothers and founders of the Missouri Synod were brought on similar yet unique paths to the faith. Walther and Loehe were affected by pietism in different ways. For Walther, it was Jesus *and* a particular form and process of conversion. Sihler was a religious liberal, a student of Friedrich Schleiermacher. Thus it was Jesus *and* subjective pious sentiments (which he failed pitifully!). They were all finally struck by their own depravity and need and were directed to Jesus. The "Jesus *and* . . ." dross melted away. They found *Jesus only* in the Sacred Scriptures. They found in the Scriptures Jesus' own voice, the voice of the Shepherd. *Jesus only*. And when they turned to read the Lutheran Confessions, they recognized the biblical confession: *Jesus only*. And it grabbed their hearts and transfixed them.

Wyneken, Walther, and Sihler went through severe trials prior to the Synod's founding. Scandal. Depression. Illness. Hardships. Death. Division. Theological error. One by one, every "Jesus *and* . . ." was knocked away. "I count all things dung next to the surpassing greatness of knowing Jesus Christ as my Savior, and being found in Him not having a righteousness of my own which comes from the law, but the righteousness of God that comes through faith" (see Philippians 3:8–9). *Solus Christus!* Only Jesus.

"There is no other name . . . given among men by which we must be saved" save Jesus Christ (Acts 4:12). How does God accomplish this salvation? Only through a cross. "The Son of Man must be glorified." It was obtained by the cross, and it's delivered through lowly cruciform means (humble preaching, voice, water, bread and wine, a catechism, a humble pastor, a lowly congregation, sinful people, whether they are on an urban corner, a desolate snow-swept landscape, or in a tiny church).

Throughout the past half century, we have been disabused of our pride, arrogance, and self-assured certainty. Demographic trends, the lowest birth and marriage rates in the history of the United States, the largest rejection of all and any religion in the history of the United States. These and many other things are tearing away from us all the "Jesus *and* . . ." scaffolding we once leaned upon. The state has become hostile to Christian belief. The entertainment industry is hostile. The university is hostile. The culture is hostile. Our children are bombarded 24/7. "Lord, to whom shall we go? You have the words of eternal life" (John 6:68). What do we have? *Only Jesus.*

Our times are intense and unique. But the basic battle has been the same from the beginning of the church. The Missouri Synod is not some "world conquering," "ever triumphant," "culture transforming," "missionary powerhouse." The Missouri Synod is first and foremost 6,000 congregations, most small, where the faithful—battered by the crosses and trials of life—give and receive Jesus. We are sinners redeemed, daily reminded by our sins that we need Jesus, *only Jesus.*

The Missouri Synod is pastors, teachers, people, and missionaries who know Jesus and share Jesus in their families, with their friends, and in every facet of their lives. "We cannot but speak of what we have seen and heard" (Acts 4:20). This witness, individually and corporately, is marked above all by Jesus' cross, Jesus' words of forgiveness, and Jesus' own compassion. Sinners telling sinners about a Savior. *Only Jesus.* "When I am lifted up from the earth, [I] will draw all people to Myself" (John 12:32). That is Jesus' *only* mission. And that is our *only* mission. It's the *only* reason we exist and the *only* reason the world continues to exist. *Only Jesus.*

> Whoever loves his life loses it, and whoever hates his life in this world will keep it for eternal life. If anyone serves Me, he must follow Me; and where I am, there will My servant be also. (John 12:25–26)

> There is no other name under heaven given among men by which we must be saved. (Acts 4:12)

Our future is in Your hands. Humble us, heavenly Father; only in doing so, let us be Your witnesses.

In the name of the Father and of the Son and of the Holy Spirit. Amen.

The Certain Gospel

....

St. Paul's Letter to the Galatians is a *tour de force* of certainty for every Christian. It both describes and produces certainty in the Gospel of free forgiveness in Jesus Christ. Christian certainty is not found in persons, feelings, sentiments, reason, positions, human actions, laws, social arrangements, or even the Ten Commandments. These all must serve the Gospel. They remain in their own created domain, functioning as God intended them to function. They have no claim on the Christian conscience. They were neither intended nor have any right to be the source of certainty in our relationship with almighty God, Father, Son, and Holy Spirit. As soon as they make any claim for or against our eternal salvation, they must be put back in their place, even ignored. Why?

St. Paul gets to the crux of the matter at Galatians 2:16: "A person is not justified by works of the law but through faith in Jesus Christ." On this verse, Luther commented: "A Christian is not someone who has no sin or feels no sin; he is someone to whom, because of his faith in Christ, God does not impute his sin." Luther continued: "The first step in Christianity is the preaching of repentance and the knowledge of oneself. The second step is this: If you want to be saved, your salvation does not come from works; but God has sent His only Son into the world that we might live through Him. He was crucified and died for you and bore your sins in His own body."[1]

Can and should a Christian be absolutely certain of God's favor today, in this life, here and now? And can and should a Christian also be absolutely certain that upon death, the soul of the believer is

---

1   *Lectures on Galatians*, AE 26:133, 126.

in the presence of Jesus to await a bodily resurrection, including a new heaven and a new earth? *Absolutely yes!*

We need only read the first few verses from Paul's letter: "Paul, an apostle—not from men nor through man, but through Jesus Christ and God the Father, who raised Him from the dead—and all the brothers who are with me, To the churches of Galatia" (Galatians 1:1–2).

The Galatian Christians were troubled by some who asserted that to be saved all non-Jewish Christians had to believe in Christ *and* keep the laws of Old Testament Judaism (including the Ten Commandments) *and* be circumcised. Over against all of this, Paul drew a firm line in the sand: It was either all Christ, or it was nothing. It is not Christ *plus* the Law that obtains salvation. In fact, anything other than Christ *alone* damns (Galatians 1:6–9). By what authority did Paul claim this? The authority of the risen Savior, Jesus Christ, through God the Father. Paul received this Gospel from Jesus by revelation, and he was mandated to preach it.

> Grace to you and peace from God our Father and the Lord Jesus Christ, who gave Himself for our sins to deliver us from the present evil age, according to the will of our God and Father, to whom be the glory forever and ever. Amen. (Galatians 1:3–5)

"Grace and peace," Paul writes to the troubled Galatian churches. Paul does not say, "Do good works and feel holy enough to please God." That would only bring uncertainty or damnable self-righteousness. Grace is God's free favor toward us because of what Jesus has already done for us. The "art" of being a Christian is the realization that sins constantly plague me and that I constantly need Jesus.

Do you want certainty? Then look to Jesus.

> For until our death, Satan will never stop attacking all the doctrines of the Creed in us. . . . Begin where Christ began—in the Virgin's womb, in the manger, and at His mother's breasts. For this purpose He came down, was born, lived among men, suffered, was crucified, and died, so that in every possible way He might present Himself

to our sight. He wanted us to fix the gaze of our hearts upon Himself and thus to prevent us from clambering into heaven and speculating about the Divine Majesty.[2]

"Speculation about the Divine Majesty" is all the rage in this world. Just about every non-Christian I talk with has cooked up some personal homemade religion. The last one I heard was that "God is probably an alien from some other planet." No one takes the Law seriously. No one has an answer for the depravity and evil of the world. No one knows the severity of the Law's demands. No one can give peace to troubled consciences. No one knows anything of God's *grace* in Jesus Christ.

Luther wrote: "This Wittenberg of ours is a holy village, and we are truly holy, because we have been baptized, communed, taught, and called by God; we have the works of God among us, that is, the Word and the sacraments, and these make us holy."[3]

Paul's letter to the Galatians shaped the Lutheran Reformation tremendously. The Reformation was about certainty in Christ, rather than uncertainty in self-righteousness. As Paul and Luther clearly taught, such certainty produces a good conscience, faith to fight sin daily, strength to love family and neighbors, and a compulsion to tell others this marvelous Good News.

Yet we know that a person is not justified by works of the law but through faith in Jesus Christ, so we also have believed in Christ Jesus, in order to be justified by faith in Christ and not by works of the law, because by works of the law no one will be justified. (Galatians 2:16)

---

2   *Lectures on Galatians*, AE 26:31, 29.
3   *Lectures on Galatians*, AE 26:24–25.

Encouragement to the 2020 Chicago Life March

· ·

E nough's enough! Sixty-one million is enough.

The canards won't hold!

If you see a video ultrasound of your child or grandchild, even moving in the womb, tell me why another such child, genetically distinct from its mother, should be denied the right to live, be dismembered and thrown in the trash.

If we are doing prenatal surgery on an unborn child in one operating theater and dismembering one in another, this does not make sense, does it?

Sixty-one million is enough! Don't you think? The canards won't hold!

The life movement is diverse; it's not a lockstep group of fanatic automatons. I guarantee you that in this crowd alone you will find the most diverse views on all current and hot button moral and political and even religious issues. If there is one issue that begs to unite us all, it is the issue of equal rights for all, liberty for all, justice for all, and the pursuit of happiness for all!

The canards won't hold!

Have you had an abortion? You will not find in this group hatred or anger or hostility. Ask about the experience of those in this group who have had abortions. There are organizations represented here today who specialize in caring for exactly you.

The canards won't hold!

This community is more pro-women than any other. Are you facing an unplanned pregnancy? You will in this community find assistance every step of the way. You'll find physical help; you'll find housing; you'll find food; you'll find counseling; you'll find adoption services; you'll find services to help you keep the baby, if you wish.

Slavery was the "original sin" of this country. It was a denial of the truth enshrined in our founding documents: "All men are created equal . . . with certain inalienable rights." These are rights not granted by any government; they are rights given us by our Creator and only assured by governments.

The martyr for this truth, Abraham Lincoln, said, "My ancient faith teaches me that 'all men are created equal' and that there can be no moral right in connection with one man's making a slave of another" (Peoria, 1854). It took 600,000 violent deaths, and a century, for the nation to begin to come to its senses. It took another century of injustice and persecution and death for the nation to begin to live the truth of its founding.

Sixty-one million is enough, isn't it?

My ancient faith tells me all men are created equal.

My ancient faith tells me all are equally accountable to and valuable to God Almighty.

My ancient Christian faith tells me of a God of mercy. "The blood of Jesus [God's] Son cleanses us from all sin" (1 John 1:7).

My ancient faith tells me that Jesus is the King of second chances! He is the King of hope.

Gospel Courage against the Sin of Racism

....

Racism is a reality. In our ever more sin-sick world, incidents such as the crazed and premeditated murders in Buffalo (May 2022)—which took the lives of beloved fathers, mothers, sons, and daughters, just because they were Black—plague us. We are reminded of the racist sins of the previous generations even as we face present racism. The sin of racism is not simply something "out there." Sin, including racism, is an ever-present reality to which we are all susceptible because of our sinful nature. Everyone has the sinful propensity to prejudge and mistreat other children of God based upon their skin color, culture, or some other difference we perceive. But "God shows no partiality" (Acts 10:34; Romans 2:11). Act 17:26

Many, including some in the LCMS, have embraced a response to racism similar to that advocated by Ibram X. Kendi in his 2019 book *How to Be an Antiracist* (New York: One World 2019). In his book, Kendi asserts that the claim to be not racist or to state "I am not racist" is insufficient and even betrays a racist attitude. One must be "antiracist" by actively opposing racist policies.

Kendi casts a very wide net. He asserts that aspects of President Lyndon Johnson's "Great Society" promoted racist policies. He asserts that the great W. E .B. Du Bois promoted a racist idea when he argued that Black Americans should assimilate into the larger culture. He asserts that Presidents Bill Clinton and Barack Obama promoted racist views when they called on the Black community to concentrate on creating stronger families (a challenge shared by all of us). Kendi also asserts that "tough on crime" legislation and efforts to defend religious freedom are inherently racist.

Kendi asserts that "homophobia" and "transphobia" are racist. The church does not fear homosexual or trans people. The church preaches repentance and faith to all people according to God's Word. We are all sinners. We all need the forgiveness of Jesus promised and delivered in the Gospel.

Kendi says "patriarchy" is racist (that includes church bodies such as the LCMS that have a male-only clergy). Women who support such systems are also racist. Any refusal to support the current global warming agenda is likewise racist because, he opines, the effects of global warming most intensely affect peoples of the Global South. Kendi says standardized tests are racist. He also accuses of racism any Black person who does not concur with his approach. In a video, he asserted that Christian missions are illegitimate since they are the attempt of white missionaries to force Africans and others to acquiesce to white standards of morality.

My deepest concern is that Kendi promotes a virulently anti-Christian philosophy. Can you imagine St. Paul preaching in the sex-crazed world of the Gentiles without the call to repentance for sexual immorality (Romans 1–2)? (See also Acts 15, where the apostolic council wisely refused to impose the Mosaic law upon converts but urged abstaining from immoral sexual sins.) There is no room in Kendi's "antiracism" for God's Law or the one truth of the Gospel for all people. There is no room for the clear teaching of Holy Scripture on matters of marriage and sexuality.

What bothers me most is that this philosophy teaches that every Bible-believing Christian, or anyone who holds virtually any conservative view, is racist. That is not true nor acceptable. Least of all is it acceptable in the church's schools and institutions. Should Kendi be read and studied? To be sure, since his voice is popular and influential. But we must set forth biblical truth on these and all matters. We need to articulate and act in a truly God-pleasing manner that condemns all sin, including racism, and articulates God's love in Christ for all.

We must continue to treat all people as God's creatures, taking seriously sin and grace. Kendi does not offer a prescription for the end of racism. In the end, he increases it. What he offers is a substitute religion that brooks no dissent from his views.

There is no one Christian policy or position on (much of) education, crime, family, poverty, immigration, global warming, etc. That's why the LCMS makes few statements on policy matters but rather urges Christians to be good citizens and to act justly when they participate in the secular realm. Christians are free to make decisions that they believe are for the good of the world.

Some ask what the LCMS is doing about racism. The most important thing we do and have done is teach our people that racism is sinful and that God loves all people in Christ. Since the 1950s, the LCMS has specifically rejected discrimination and racism no fewer than thirty-nine times in convention. The Synod has officially rejected segregated housing and many other racist practices. Have we always lived up to God's intention in this matter? Certainly not. God's Law demands perfection and always condemns. But we continue to call all to repent, to be forgiven in Christ, and to move forward in love and respect, to act as responsible Christians and citizens. I urge you all to read *Racism and the Church* by our own Commission on Theology and Church Relations (at lcms.org/social-issues/racism).

I also encourage you to buy *Luther's Small Catechism with Explanation* (2017 edition) from Concordia Publishing House. In the explanation section that addresses the Fifth Commandment (You shall not murder), you will find compelling texts of Scripture that preclude all violence and encourage love and care for our neighbor. Here's what the catechism explanation on the Fifth Commandment says about racism in particular:

> **Question 62. How does this commandment apply to some specific issues today?**
>
> **E. It forbids hating, despising, or slandering other groups of people (prejudice, racism, and so forth).**

Acts 17:26 [God] made from one man every nation of mankind to live on all the face of the earth, having determined allotted periods and boundaries of their dwelling place.

James 2:1 My brothers, show no partiality as you hold the faith in our Lord Jesus Christ.

1 John 3:15 Everyone who hates his brother is a murderer, and you know that no murderer has eternal life abiding in him.

Revelation 5:9 And they sang a new song . . . saying, "You were slain, and by Your blood You ransomed people for God from every tribe and language and people and nation."

Our teaching on racism and other issues is rooted deeply in the Gospel of Jesus Christ. In fact, the Bible contains the strongest anti-racist teaching in the history of the world:

1.   Each and every person is descended from Adam, who was made in the image of God. We are one race.

2.   Each and every person has the exact same problem; original sin is the great equalizer (Romans 3:23; 5:12–14).

3.   Each and every human being's worth has been established by nothing less than the very blood of Jesus Christ (Mark 10:45; 1 John 1:5–7).

4.   Each and every person is dearly loved by God (John 3:16; 1 John 1:7–9; 1 Timothy 2:4).

With 5,700 active pastors and 20,000 teachers and other church workers daily preaching and teaching that violence and discrimination are sinful, even with our weaknesses, the LCMS is a powerhouse of clear teaching about love and respect for all people.

I am going to ask some of our theologians to give a biblical response to critical race theory and to equip our people with resources to navigate these challenging times. We are already working with one of our Concordias to create a curriculum that will address unity and diversity from a thoroughly biblical perspective; once ready, we will make it available to other Concordias too.

Racism is real. Hatred of other people—for whatever reason—is real. Competing, sometimes anti-Christian responses to these problems, uninformed by the Law's diagnosis of the real human predicament and by the Gospel's solution to every human shortcoming, will ultimately fail. Let this encourage you: only the church has the real solution to racism or any other societal ill or human misdeed. Jesus died for all people. Every baptized person is a son of God by faith (Galatians 3:25–26). *all in = to all people is racism*

The church cannot follow the world. The church should not become embroiled in secular policy debates when the Bible does not clearly mandate one Christian response. The Christian lives in two realms, state and church. Christians recognize this country has a tragic history of state-sponsored racism. Christians as citizens should involve themselves in the secular/political world as appropriate to their vocations. Christians should vote. Christians will not always come to the same conclusions on these matters. Christians walk according to Micah 6:8: "What does the LORD require of you but to do justice, and to love kindness, and to walk humbly with your God?"

Meanwhile, the church has *the* anti-racist policy—the Gospel.

Faithful
unto Death

....

The United States Supreme Court ruling *Obergefell v. Hodges* legalized same-sex marriage in all fifty states in 2015. This significant ruling influenced our nation and the world in many aspects of civilization and life. It placed the law of the land in direct contradiction to reason, natural law, and the divinely revealed will of our Creator.

But now, the recent Supreme Court decision *Bostock v. Clayton County* pits the law and force of the federal government against orthodox Christians. The Civil Rights Act of 1964 forbids employment discrimination on the basis of "race, color, religion, sex or national origin." In *Bostock*, the court injected transgender and homosexual practices into the word "sex" from the 1964 ruling. This truly preposterous reading of the law loads meaning into a term which, when the law was made in 1964, was clearly intended to mean male or female. Again, like *Roe v. Wade* and *Obergefell v. Hodges*, the court has usurped the authority of the legislative branch and made up laws by reinterpreting texts to say something they were never intended to say.

We in the Missouri Synod are familiar with this manner of interpreting texts. This was the basic issue in the 1960s and '70s in our church body. Do the texts of the Bible mean what they say, and are they clear and authoritative as intended by the divine Author? Or may they be deconstructed and filled with all sorts of political or philosophical meaning at odds with what the texts say?

We believe, based on the clear and unchanging teachings of the Bible, that all human beings are created in the image of God (Genesis 1:26). We believe that all are loved by God (John 3:16).

We believe that "all have sinned and fall short of the glory of God" (Romans 3:23). We believe the sacrificial death and resurrection of Christ is for all (2 Corinthians 5:19). We are thankful that Jesus "receives sinners and eats with them" (Luke 15:2). The Law calls all of us to repentance and to faith in Christ. And we are all to "bear fruit in keeping with repentance" (Matthew 3:8).

Christians want all people to be treated with dignity. The founding documents of this nation guarantee human rights, such as "life, liberty and the pursuit of happiness." But we are now entering new territory. The fundamental teaching that God has made us male and female; that the sexes are not interchangeable; and that lesbian, gay, bisexual, and transsexual uses of our created male and female sexuality are not in accord with divine will is clearly and repeatedly revealed in Holy Scripture (Romans 1:18–31). The Supreme Court has now ruled against this biblical view.

The only question remaining is what of current law—for example, the Religious Freedom Restoration Act of 1991, *Hosanna-Tabor Evangelical Lutheran Church and School v. Equal Employment Opportunity Commission*, or the First Amendment's "free exercise clause"—will leave us room to operate our churches, schools, universities, and institutions according to our Christian doctrine and consciences. What if a male parochial school janitor shows up one day dressed as a woman? What if a non-LCMS professor at one of our universities does so? What if a Concordia university coach has surgery to "change genders" (as if this were possible)? We have established our churches, schools, and institutions so that we can inculcate biblical values in our youth and share those values with others. We must not compromise with the world. Jesus said, "If salt has lost its taste . . . it is no longer good for anything except to be thrown out and trampled under people's feet" (Matthew 5:13). As Paul teaches in Galatians, the church that cannot say "no" cannot say "yes" either (Galatians 1:6–10). The church that cannot speak the curse of the Law cannot speak the Gospel. Lose the divine Law, and you lose the Gospel too.

Hermann Sasse spoke in 1930 to a context in Germany eerily similar to our own. He was commenting on "governing authority," based on St. Paul's Letter to the Romans: "Let every person be subject to the governing authorities. For there is no authority except from God, and those that exist have been instituted by God" (Romans 13:1). Sasse observed that "a governing authority which knowingly or unknowingly . . . allows the norms of the law to be dictated by the so-called 'legal consciousness' of the time, sinks to the level of raw power."[1] "We must obey God rather than men" (Acts 5:29).

I suspect that we are about to see what such "raw power" of the state will mean for biblical, confessional Christians in the United States today and into the future. We have but one option: "Be faithful unto death, and I will give you the crown of life" (Revelation 2:10). This promise reveals that it's not so bad to have limited options when they are laid out by the true Lord and King. "So we can confidently say, 'The Lord is my helper; I will not fear; what can man do to me?'" (Hebrews 13:6).

---

1   Hermann Sasse, "The Social Doctrine of the Augsburg Confession and Its Significance for the Present," in *The Lonely Way* (St. Louis: Concordia Publishing House, 2001), 1:98.

The End
of Comfortable
Christianity

. . . .

The church is not and never has been a country club—though in the last century, especially in North America, it might have been confused for one. You could conduct business after the voters' meeting, unofficially govern the affairs of the city from the church parking lot, and use your Sunday morning bulletin to get a discount at the buffet. In the middle of the twentieth century, it was normal for people to be members of a Christian church. Pastors could regularly get a "clergyman's discount" at retail stores. Being a member of a Christian denomination was expected, even American. These are the halcyon days for which people pine when they lament the loss of "the good ol' days."

Those days are gone. Thanks be to God.

Recently, our good friends Bishop Juhana Pohjola of the Evangelical Lutheran Mission Diocese of Finland and Dr. Päivi Räsänen, a member of the Finnish Parliament, were on trial for charges of "hate speech" for confessing what Scripture simply and clearly teaches about God's design for marriage and the sinful nature of homosexuality. They made the great "mistake" of quoting what the Bible says in Romans 1 and other passages. The trial began on January 24, the Feast of St. Timothy. It was scheduled to conclude February 14, the Feast of St. Valentine.

Both Timothy and Valentine were martyrs. That is, they were killed for their confession of Christ. That is, they were witnesses to the Gospel by means of the shedding of their own blood. They never got clergyman's discounts or tax benefits.

Jesus promised His apostles: "You will be hated by all for My name's sake" (Matthew 10:22). He knew of the fate of His apostles when He sent them out. He knew of the persecution that would afflict His Christians for the first centuries of the Church. He knew the fate of Timothy and Valentine even before He formed them in the womb. He knew of His holy martyrs Justin, Perpetua, Felicitas, Polycarp, Cyprian, Robert Barnes, and all the others whom we commemorate throughout the Church Year. If you don't know the stories of these saints, look them up. He knew Bishop Pohjola and Member of Parliament [MP] Räsänen would stand before the Finnish courts. Thanks be to God, they were both acquitted of the evil charges brought against them, but the state could still appeal the decision. So while we do not know the end of their ordeal, their Lord knows the end.

The rest of Jesus' words to His apostles in Matthew are telling.

Behold, I am sending you out as sheep in the midst of wolves, so be wise as serpents and innocent as doves. Beware of men, for they will deliver you over to courts and flog you in their synagogues, and you will be dragged before governors and kings for My sake, to bear witness before them and the Gentiles. When they deliver you over, do not be anxious how you are to speak or what you are to say, for what you are to say will be given to you in that hour. For it is not you who speak, but the Spirit of your Father speaking through you. Brother will deliver brother over to death, and the father his child, and children will rise against parents and have them put to death, and you will be hated by all for My name's sake. But the one who endures to the end will be saved. (Matthew 10:16–22)

Christianity has never been comfortable. When the Church gets comfortable in the culture, her confession gets watered down. The proclamation of the Law is diminished, and the proclamation of the Gospel gets lost.

As goes Europe, North America soon follows. Canada already has "hate speech" laws similar to Finland's. Probably not in this generation, but maybe in the next, Christians in North America will likely have to stand before the courts just like our Finnish brother and sister. What will we say? What we have always said. Our friends in Finland at every opportunity have confessed that all humans are precious and created in the image of God, and all of us are sinful and in need of a Savior, Jesus.

We preach Christ crucified. The Church is cruciform, cross-shaped. That's not comfortable. Never has been. But we have a hope beyond the creature comforts of this life. Jesus promised persecution. And He promised resurrection.

> **Do not fear those who kill the body but cannot kill the soul. Rather fear him who can destroy both soul and body in hell. Are not two sparrows sold for a penny? And not one of them will fall to the ground apart from your Father. But even the hairs of your head are all numbered. Fear not, therefore; you are of more value than many sparrows. So everyone who acknowledges Me before men, I also will acknowledge before My Father who is in heaven, but whoever denies Me before men, I also will deny before My Father who is in heaven.** (Matthew 10:28–33)

Jesus rose triumphant from the grave. He will not abandon to the grave those who belong to Him. He will raise His martyrs, His confessors, His saints from all time and all places. Body and soul back together. All the elect will be gathered into His new heavens and new earth to life in perfect bliss in the presence of the triune God and of one another. This hope is what emboldened and encouraged the martyrs. It is what emboldens and encourages Bishop Pohjola and MP Räsänen. It will be what emboldens and encourages us or our children or our grandchildren when we face persecution.

The era of comfortable country-club Christianity is over. And I'm okay with that. As the church faces increasing harassment in the West, which will soon turn to persecution, it will sharpen our confession of Christ crucified for sinners. It will fix our hopes forward to the certain resurrection that awaits all the Lord's Church.

A decade ago the official (once Lutheran) Finnish Church defrocked Bishop Pohjola and expelled his vibrant and growing congregation from its building for refusing the unbiblical practice of female pastors and the state church's confusion on sex. What happened? They lost a beautiful building but soon rented a space from Seventh-day Adventists. Now the Evangelical Lutheran Mission Diocese of Finland (the LCMS's newest partner church) has planted forty congregations. When I ask my friend the bishop how things are going, he responds, "Every time they attack us, we grow."

Be bold. Be courageous. Nothing can diminish our hope. Nothing can daunt our confession.

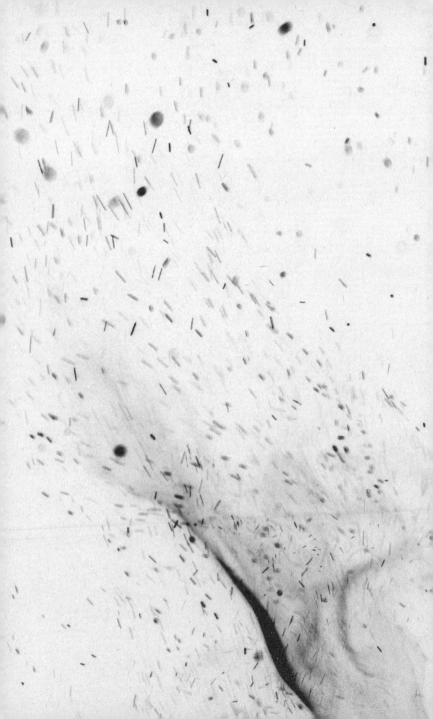

PART III

Courage to Die

Every one of us is mortal, so what good is having the courage to die?

We might do better asking the question from the other direction. What good is it to face death without courage? To cower night and day under a thundercloud of dread? To be subject to seizures of fear whenever your thoughts wander toward life's inevitable conclusion? How can a person be anything but a slave to death's despotic terror without some real hope?

Every one of us will fall and die. But our Lord Jesus lays His hand on us and says, "Fear not, I am the first and the last, and the living one. I died, and behold I am alive forevermore, and I have the keys of Death and Hades" (Revelation 1:17–18).

The Christian's confidence in the face of death is one of the greatest confessions he can make in his life. Her serene departure from this life, confiding in her Savior, testifies to her trust that this end is not really the end. This little miracle of peace is one each of us has an opportunity, by God's grace, to manifest for His glory and the good of all people. *Fear not.*

The Problem
of Death

·····················

"P astor, I've got a problem." I'll never forget that statement and the 90-year-old man who said it to me while I visited him in an aged care facility.

"What's wrong, Henry?" I replied.

"Pastor, I can't die."

Henry was done. He felt useless. He wasn't in his own home. He wanted to see Jesus. Can you imagine that strange frustration? None of us can until we've faced it ourselves. Henry knew Jesus then. Now he knows his Savior face-to-face.

What even to say to such a profound saint? Answer: The important words are not mine, but the Lord's. "In the stead and by the command of my Lord Jesus Christ I forgive you all your sins." "Our Father who art in heaven . . ." "Take, eat. . . . Take, drink; this is the true blood of our Lord and Savior Jesus Christ, shed for the forgiveness of your sins." "Lord, now lettest Thou Thy servant depart in peace according to Thy word." "The Lord bless you and keep you. The Lord make His face shine upon you and be gracious unto you. The Lord lift up His countenance upon you and give you peace. Amen."

I muttered a few thoughts. "Henry, I know exactly why you're still alive. It's your job right now to show your family how a Christian man dies believing in Jesus." And the Lord preserved old Henry and gave him all he needed to do just that. What a joy and honor was mine as his pastor to care for him and comfort him at that crucial time in his long life.

Pastors see a lot of death and a lot of funerals. Sometimes it's all too much, burying friends and dear brothers and sisters in Christ one has known for decades. Familiarity with death never makes it easier, but ministering to the dying so often takes away the unfamiliarity of what's coming next. I suppose it helps pastors hold it together when others are falling apart. Pastors share the certainty of the resurrection of Christ as they are able to be present, calm, and helpful to those facing the death of a loved one.

Most LCMS congregations are small. This means that most pastors know their parishioners well and can spend significant time with the dying. It's a profound honor. I discovered something remarkable early on as a pastor. I always check the church records for a confirmation verse and use it as the sermon text, or at least as a strong theme in the funeral sermon. It's curious how often the verse fits the life of the person. I recall thinking for years that those old pastors really knew what they were doing when they chose verses for each child. I'm sure they did. But then it struck me. I became convinced that because "the word of God is living and active, sharper than any two-edged sword" (Hebrews 4:12), this very Word, placed upon a person in blessing, shapes lives. You will not convince me otherwise.

One of the greatest blessings of being a pastor is that people invite you into their lives to speak God's Word at the best times but also at the worst and saddest. It's a profound honor to do both for the same people. Funerals are often sad, sometimes tragic. But we have Christ. The funeral service in our *Lutheran Service Book* brings Jesus at every turn. The hymns sung at the deathbed and then at the funeral strengthen, encourage, and point to Christ. Indeed, the truly valuable hymns have something to say in the hour of death. The Word of God and its strong testimony to Jesus and His resurrection is our only hope. And Jesus brings joy, even in death and sorrow.

> **But we do not want you to be uninformed, brothers, about those who are asleep, that you may not grieve as others do who have no hope. For since we believe that Jesus died and rose again, even so, through Jesus, God will bring with Him those who have fallen asleep.** (1 Thessalonians 4:13–14)

The "problem of death" becomes a great opportunity to confess Jesus, to show one's loved ones how to die in Christ and how to live in the certainty of a resurrection just like His.

In the Hour
of Death ... Jesus!

....

When a Christian passes from this vale of tears peacefully and without great struggle or pain, it's a blessing. But even in those cases, death is not pretty. It's horrible.

People often rally near the end. Eyes may suddenly open. A dying person may respond to a loved one's words or affection. I think it's God's creative genius to allow final words, final forgiveness, final consolation in Christ. Breathing is often labored toward the end. The "death rattle" was more common at one time, but is now more rare as medication reduces or eliminates it. Hospice and medical care can lessen discomfort and pain greatly.

How many times I've seen loved ones, friends, parishioners weaken to the point of a few shallow last breaths, fall completely still, mouth ajar, paling now ... in moments turning to the morbid glaze of death. Last kisses. Last prayers. Last "I love yous." Hands held as the body grows cold. What a profound privilege and honor it is to share these moments with dear ones, and as a pastor with Christians. A final hymn and prayers. "I Know That My Redeemer Lives." "Jesus Christ Is Risen Today." The beloved deceased was baptized, received the Sacrament, trusted in Jesus.

Sometimes death is sudden, tragic, and shockingly unexpected. Sometimes the pain of the loss of a child or a suicide is unbearable. Why? Why, Lord? Why this, Lord? Where were You, Lord? The only answers come from His revealed Word:

Come to Me, all who labor and are heavy laden, and I will give you rest. (Matthew 11:28)

Oh, the depth of the riches and wisdom and knowledge of God! How unsearchable His judgments. (Romans 11:33)

No one will snatch them out of My hand. (John 10:28)

It's such a fabulous blessing to be a Christian (and a Lutheran at that)—to have the comfort of the Word even when we do not have explanations for every death that touches us.

I've done funerals of lovely, elderly Christians whose extended family had left Christianity decades earlier. I've seen petty funeral fights, over-the-top emotional explosions, massive arguments. But Christians do not "grieve as others do who have no hope" (1 Thessalonians 4:13). Quite the contrary. We know that we shall die and live with Jesus, only to await the resurrection of the dead and a heavenly, physical eternity with Him. Mourning with the promise of comfort (Matthew 5:4) is what allows us to mourn, rather than to panic, lash out, or withdraw.

Today, people increasingly shield themselves from face-to-face experiences with death. Viewings and even funerals, once conducted in homes, are becoming less and less common (regardless of circumstances that sometimes limit these customs). The hammer of the Law strikes by death, to be sure. It is fearsome. This is the very reason to gather family around the deceased. Speaking the Word of God and the Gospel of the resurrection lets each and every person see death for what it is, and see what Christ has done for us. "Whoever believes in Me, though he die, yet shall he live" (John 11:25).

Grieving
with Hope

....

Martin Luther's wife, Katie, gave birth to six children. After 1529, there were probably another dozen or so children of a deceased sister and another sister added to the Luther household. Katie's "Aunt Lene," who had fled the monastery with Katie, was also in the house.

At any given moment, there were refugees from other countries, dignitaries, royals suffering marital troubles, and loads of students lodging in the large, old cloister that Frederick the Wise had given to Luther for his home. Luther even had a bowling alley put in at one point to offer the crowd some recreation.

Amazingly, we don't find Luther complaining about this plethora of people. He enjoyed it. Katie managed the whole thing. But it is noteworthy that in Luther's day, with limited medical treatment and catastrophic diseases such as the plague, death at home was a close reality.

Katie gave birth to their second child, Elizabeth, on December 10, 1527—during an outbreak of the plague in Wittenberg. The poor child died the following August. Luther was devastated:

> **My baby daughter, little Elizabeth, has passed away. It is amazing what a sick heart . . . she has left to me, so much has grief for her overcome me. Never before would I have believed that a father's heart could have such tender feelings for his child. Do pray to the Lord for me.**[1]

---

1   Letter to Nicholas Hausmann, AE 49:203.

Luther's pain was even worse when he lost his teenage daughter, Magdelena, in September 1542:

> When his daughter was in the agony of death, he fell on his knees before the bed and, weeping bitterly, prayed that God might will to save her. Thus she gave up the ghost in the arms of her father. Her mother was in the same room, but farther from the bed on account of her grief. It was after the ninth hour on the Wednesday after the Fifteenth Sunday after Trinity in the year 1542.[2]

Several references tell of Luther's great struggle, the struggle we all face in times of death.

With the recent death of my own brother, my family is facing this struggle now. We know the certainty of eternal life in Christ, freely given, and we have the sure hope of the resurrection of the body. Yet the pain of loss—a real, visceral pain, particularly for my parents—is, frankly, overwhelming at times. "I believe; help my unbelief!" (Mark 9:24).

> When [Magdelena] died, [Luther] said, "I am joyful in spirit but I am sad according to the flesh. The flesh doesn't take kindly to this. The separation troubles me above measure. It's strange to know that she is surely at peace and that she is well off there, very well off, and yet to grieve so much!"[3]

As the coffin was taken from the home, Luther commented:

> "I've sent a saint to heaven—yes, a living saint. Would that our death might be like this!" . . . Again, turning to others, [Luther] said, "Do not be sorrowful. I have sent a saint to heaven. In fact, I have now sent two of them."[4]

I've been around a great deal of death as a pastor. I always try to stay at the death watch in homes or hospitals. It's always difficult.

2   *Table Talk* no. 5496, AE 54:431.
3   *Table Talk* no. 5498, AE 54:432.
4   *Table Talk* no. 5499, AE 54:432–33.

Watching my own dear brother pass from time to eternity was exponentially more difficult, and remains so. He died in Christ. I believe in Christ and the truth of His promises: "I go to prepare a place for you" (John 14:2).

Then why is this so painful?

"Jesus wept" (John 11:35). That's the shortest verse in the Bible. And it's odd.

Jesus *knew* that He would raise Lazarus. He *knew* the joy that would soon overcome Mary and Martha and the family. Yet He, the Son of God, grieved the horror of death. Because Jesus grieved the loss of the precious life of His friend, we know that grieving is not, in and of itself, sinful.

To be sure, sin is shot through our grieving (with doubt, fear, and anger) because sin is shot through each of us! But still, with repentant hearts as Christians, death invites us to grieve the loss of a precious person—a gift to us, a life, which has meant so much.

What a blessing to know Jesus. My brother told me in his last days, "I'm not afraid to die."

Like Luther then, and all of us at some time, my family was in deep grief for a while. My brother's life on this earth has closed and will not be opened to us again until the resurrection. But note what Paul says. Now we grieve, and it's good that we do. But Paul distinguishes between those who grieve and those grieving who "have no hope":

For since we believe that Jesus died and rose again, even so, through Jesus, God will bring with Him those who have fallen asleep. (1 Thessalonians 4:14)

The Glorious
Blessing
of Christ's
Resurrection

....

Jesus repeatedly told His inner circle that He would die and rise again. "The Son of Man is about to be delivered into the hands of men, and they will kill Him, and He will be raised on the third day" (Matthew 17:22–23). According to Jesus' own words, He offered Himself as a substitute. "For even the Son of Man came not to be served but to serve, and to give His life as a ransom for many" (Mark 10:45). This happened in fulfillment of Old Testament prophecy. "The LORD has laid on Him the iniquity of us all" (Isaiah 53:6). "He shall bear their iniquities" (Isaiah 53:11). John the Baptizer pointed to Jesus and said, "Behold, the Lamb of God, who takes away the sin of the world!" (John 1:29). In one of the most startling passages in the New Testament, St. Paul, the Lord's own apostle, wrote: "For our sake [God the Father] made Him [Christ] to be sin who knew no sin, so that in Him we might become the righteousness of God" (2 Corinthians 5:21).

How do we know the resurrection happened? The power of the Word of God, proclaiming forgiveness in Christ by faith, brings its own conviction. The New Testament mentions many "witnesses" to the historic fact of the resurrection of Christ (Acts 1:22). St. Paul says,

> Christ died for our sins in accordance with the Scriptures,[1] that He was buried, that He was raised on the third day in accordance with the Scriptures,[2] and He appeared to Cephas,[3] then to the twelve. Then He appeared to more than five hundred brothers at one time, most of whom are still alive, though some have fallen asleep. Then He appeared to James, then to all the apostles. Last of all, as to one untimely born, He appeared also to me. (1 Corinthians 15:3–8)

Paul prefaced this passage with, "I delivered to you as of first importance what I also received." Paul "hands over" the "tradition" (v. 3). These are factual, historical markers of the resurrection. I find it unendingly significant that while opponents of Jesus contested His resurrection from the beginning (Matthew 27:62–66), no one from within the group of Jesus' followers, like all those Paul noted above, ever came forward with an alternative version. There is simply no record of someone present who later says, "I was actually there, and a follower of Jesus. It did not happen the way Paul and the apostles and the evangelists wrote it."

This resurrection has many ramifications for us. The sin of the world has been atoned for. Paul puts it starkly and dramatically. Jesus "was delivered up for our trespasses and raised for our justification" (Romans 4:25). Jesus' resurrection is the grand absolution for the sins of the world. And there are other such dramatic passages: "In Christ God was reconciling the world to Himself, not counting their trespasses against them, and entrusting to us the message of reconciliation" (2 Corinthians 5:19). The "big event" happened in the death and resurrection of Christ. Righteousness and salvation have been obtained, won, paid for. How is this blessing appropriated by each of us? By faith. As one Lutheran pastor put it: "Although the air surrounds you on all sides, yet it will do you no good if your lungs do not inhale it." Faith grabs hold of the blessings of Christ—indeed,

---

1   E.g., Isaiah 53.
2   Cf. Matthew 12:38–42, on "the sign of Jonah."
3   I.e., Peter; cf. Luke 24:34 and John 21:15–19.

of Christ Himself. Or perhaps it is better to say, in faith Christ grabs hold of us.

If nothing that happened today could change tomorrow, what would it give you freedom to do today? That sounds like the start of a terrible self-help book, but think of it more like the movie *Groundhog Day*. Every day, Bill Murray's character could do whatever he wanted because he knew the next day was going to be February 2 all over again.

That's what resurrection does. The future is guaranteed. No matter what happens in this life, whatever trials and suffering we will have to endure, nothing changes the end of the story. Our future is already written. It belongs to Jesus. He is risen; so shall we arise on the day of His return.

All the crosses and trials that afflict us today will be left in the grave at the resurrection. All the suffering and heartache will stay in the dirt. All the brokenness and frailty will decompose with the casket.

Then I saw a new heaven and a new earth, for the first heaven and the first earth had passed away, and the sea was no more. And I saw the holy city, new Jerusalem, coming down out of heaven from God, prepared as a bride adorned for her husband. And I heard a loud voice from the throne saying, "Behold, the dwelling place of God is with man. He will dwell with them, and they will be His people, and God Himself will be with them as their God. He will wipe away every tear from their eyes, and death shall be no more, neither shall there be mourning, nor crying, nor pain anymore, for the former things have passed away." (Revelation 21:1–4)

Bodies and souls knit back together perfectly. No more mourning nor crying nor pain. The former things are the former things. They will have passed away for good. God will dwell with us, His redeemed people. He will be with us as our God. Death shall be no more.

The Church lives with this courage and confidence every single day. Each Christian lives with this courage and confidence every single day. The afflictions of this life are temporary. Resurrection is forever. Take courage.

The significance of Christ's resurrection runs through the New Testament like a glorious golden thread entwined with the means of grace. *Baptism* connects us to Christ's death and resurrection (Romans 6)! Peter says, "Baptism, which corresponds to this, now saves you, not as a removal of dirt from the body but as an appeal to God for a good conscience, through the resurrection of Jesus Christ" (1 Peter 3:21). Baptism is that "appeal," which is a result of the resurrection! The resurrected Christ delivers *the Keys* to His disciples: "If you forgive the sins of any, they are forgiven" (John 20:23). Speak forgiveness! Speak resurrection! Jesus said of those whom the Father gives Him, and who thus believe in Him, "I will raise him up on the last day!" (John 6:39, 44). And in a grand reference to the *Lord's Supper*, Jesus says, "Whoever feeds on My flesh and drinks My blood has eternal life, and I will raise him up on the last day" (John 6:54).

Finally, St. Paul wrote: "But in fact Christ has been raised from the dead, the firstfruits of those who have fallen asleep" (1 Corinthians 15:20). It is the bedrock teaching of the New Testament that Christ is the first one raised, and we, too, shall be raised from the dead at the Last Day. "Sleep" is not some pie-in-the-sky euphemism for the horror of death. No, death for us Christians, as Luther described it, shall be like falling asleep and then waking refreshed from a short nap. Luther, of course, in no way denies that when our spirits leave our bodies, we are with Jesus ("Today you will be with Me in paradise," Luke 23:43). "For as in Adam all die, so also in Christ shall all be made alive. But each in his own order: Christ the firstfruits, then at His coming those who belong to Christ" (1 Corinthians 15:22–23).

What a glorious blessing is Christ's resurrection!

Witnesses
to the Resurrection

· ·

The word *witness* in the New Testament is extremely important. After the ascension of Jesus, Peter gathered the apostles (and the broader number of some 120 disciples) and informed the group that Judas, having betrayed Christ and committed suicide, must be replaced. His "office" had to be filled. Peter said,

> So one of the men who have accompanied us during all the time that the Lord Jesus went in and out among us, beginning from the baptism of John until the day when He was taken up from us—one of these men must become with us a witness to His resurrection. (Acts 1:21–22)

Jesus had told His disciples: "And you also will bear witness, because you have been with Me from the beginning" (John 15:27). The apostles were sent by Christ to bear witness to the world (Matthew 28:19; Acts 1:8). They bore witness in a legal sense, telling others what they had actually seen and heard of Jesus (1 John 1). Some of them bore witness by writing Gospels (Matthew and John) or writing down the witness of an apostle (Mark for Peter; Luke for Paul).

This witness of the apostles has always been tremendous assurance to me over against the views of liberal theologians from the past two centuries. These radicals denied that Jesus said almost everything attributed to Him in the New Testament, that He performed miracles, and even the resurrection itself. In contrast to these scholars' canards, I evaluate the witness of Jesus' closest followers.

First, liberal scholars liked to highlight that some early Jewish accounts claim that Jesus' disciples stole His body and claimed a resurrection. Liberal theologians also claimed that the church composed the Gospels as a grand fictional story embellished over time. These scholars taught that the Gospels were not written until well into the second century, long after the events they described. But archaeological discoveries have pushed the likely dating of the Gospels much earlier than previously thought—that is, right back into the first century. Most significant, no one from within the community of Jesus' disciples ever came forward and contested the facts claimed by the Gospels.

Second, as a young pastor I became convinced that these liberal scholars must not have had much pastoral experience. I recall ministering to a woman who was nearing her hundredth year. The congregation had been founded in 1885. This woman vividly recalled the founding pastor. In fact, she told me about a quip the pastor once made while visiting her parents' home. A container of beans was spilled, and some fell on the floor. The pastor quipped, "Jede Bohne kostet Geld!" "Every bean costs money!" If I were to speak falsely about this pastor, she would have contradicted me with a clear memory, almost a century old.

Another illustration: My father-in-law is 98 years old. His mind is still very sharp. Even now, he has vivid memories of events prior to 1930, including his congregation, Morningside Lutheran Church in Sioux City, Iowa. That's a ninety-year span. Jesus' resurrection occurred in AD 33. The writings of the New Testament were circulated throughout the church before AD 70. At that time, there were numerous people alive who had seen and heard Jesus. Many more had close relatives and friends who had witnessed Jesus' resurrection. None of them ever came forward and called the Gospels fiction.

The resurrection of Jesus is the foundation of our faith. It proves that Jesus is the Son of God. It proves that His message is true. Jesus "was delivered up for our trespasses and raised for our justification," as St. Paul put it (Romans 4:25). I believe it because I recognize that I am a sinner, and I hear in the Gospels and the rest of the Bible the voice of my Savior. I am confirmed in my trust by the fact that His witnesses did exactly as He wished: "This is the disciple who is bearing witness about these things, and who has written these things, and we know that his testimony is true" (John 21:24).

Only One Foot Remains in the Grave

....

A Christian has already been thrust into death by the very fact that he became a Christian. Wherever he may be, he occupies himself with this hourly. He expects death any moment so long as he sojourns here, because devil, world, and his own flesh give him no rest. However, he enjoys the advantage of already being out of the grave with this right leg. Moreover, he has a mighty helper who holds out His hand to him, namely, His Lord Christ; He has left the grave entirely a long time ago, and now He takes the Christian by the hand and pulls him more than halfway out of the grave; only the left foot remains in it. For his sin is already remitted and expunged, God's wrath and hell are extinguished, and he already lives fully in and with Christ with regard to his best part, which is the soul, as he partakes of eternal life. Therefore death can no longer hold him or harm him. Only the remnant, the old skin, flesh and blood, must still decay before it, too, can be renewed and follow the soul. As for the rest, we have already penetrated all the way into life, since Christ and my soul are no longer in death.[1]

Luther spoke so wonderfully about Christ's death and resurrection. The hard part is over, says Luther. Our resurrection from the dead will follow quickly and easily at the last trumpet. That is amazing comfort. Luther said that Jesus is called the Firstborn because there are more coming after Him. Jesus is called the Head.

---

1   *Commentary on 1 Corinthians 15*, AE 28:133.

And what's the most difficult part in birth? The head. But after that, the body comes quickly and easily. Jesus emerged from the grave, and we, the body, shall too.

I need comfort. So do you. The challenges upon us can feel beyond our capacity to cope. Recently, the Synod heard from a man who leads a church body of forty congregations, with a ten-year plan to plant 360 more. His church is working in a remote land—a place I've never been to, nor do I know anyone who has. A number of years ago, a Peace Corps volunteer gave this bishop a copy of *Luther's Small Catechism*. The church does not have "Lutheran" in its name, but I found its webpage. From the authority of Scripture, to justification by grace through faith, to baptismal regeneration, to Christ's body and blood in the Sacrament, to the office of the ministry, to a rejection of unbiblical ideas about the millennium, they are absolutely Lutheran. It's amazing what one catechism can do! They want to affiliate with the LCMS and need help figuring out how to train their pastors.

Meanwhile, another communication from a church body in Africa of some four million has requested formal fellowship talks, as well as missionaries to assist them. We currently have a record of twenty such church bodies (some enormous, others small) requesting formal talks. Because the officials of the Lutheran World Federation continue to try to convince Lutherans that the Bible is not clear on homosexuality, Lutherans in the global South and East are reaching out to us daily. Simply put, they want to associate with Lutherans who believe the Bible and Luther's catechism. We wish no one ill, but this is just a fact.

Our strength is not sufficient for the task. The Synod's domestic situation alone is daunting beyond belief. We don't have the capacity, the finances, the mercy funding, the missionaries. And yet, doors keep opening. We do what we can when we can. Blessings rain down upon us, despite ourselves. What Luther says is true. Only our left foot remains in the grave. Christ has done the heavy lifting, and He still does it. What joy is ours as resurrection people to participate in Christ's own great mission of seeking, finding, and delivering the lost!

Dear Jesus, give us strength for today and uphold us tomorrow. We are Yours. Thy will, not ours, be done. Amen.

Ashes to Ashes,
Dust to Dust

. . . .

How many times have I stood at an open grave and spoken these ancient words:

> **We now commit the body of our brother/sister to the ground; earth to earth, ashes to ashes, dust to dust, in the sure and certain hope of the resurrection to eternal life through our Lord Jesus Christ, who will change our lowly bodies so that they will be like His glorious body, by the power that enables Him to subdue all things to Himself.**
> (*LSB Agenda*, 130)

Hundreds of faces . . . sorrowing loved ones . . . faithful parishioners now gone . . . mourning families of suicide victims . . . vestments flapping in a frigid wind . . . unexpected deaths . . . deaths after long illness . . . many different cemeteries . . . loved ones gone. They all run together in my mind. "Ashes to ashes, dust to dust . . ."

More and more, I have a hard time looking death square in the face. It's a horrid experience, but it's also tremendously salutary. "The wages of sin is death" (Romans 6:23). Death is the curse of sin. Sin brought that curse to Adam. "You are dust, and to dust you shall return" (Genesis 3:19). We live in a world that does not take sin seriously, and it never really has.

When I see death up close, I think of Jesus. When I see a loved one's face fall in death, I recall Another who suffered horribly. I know Another who was in agony in His last hours. He could barely breathe. He was beaten, pierced and bleeding. I know Another who spoke His last words. I know Another who said to a terrible sinner who had come to believe, "Today you will be with Me in paradise" (Luke 23:43).

I know Another who said, "It is finished!" (John 19:30). I know Another whose face fell and turned white in death, whose body hung lifeless and was buried.

And we know how His story ended. Jesus rose from the grave! "The free gift of God is eternal life in Christ Jesus our Lord" (Romans 6:23)! He "was delivered up for our trespasses and raised for our justification" (Romans 4:25)!

Lent is somewhat like a Christian funeral. We must stare the awful truth of sin and death directly in the face. In fact, we must stare at it in a mirror. There's a stench to death, and there's a stench to a life filled with sin, conceit, dishonesty, idolatry, hypocrisy, lust, jealousy, greed, selfishness, and more. During Lent, we contemplate anew the depth of our sin, so great that it took the death of the Great Physician to heal us!

Like the great guitarist Doc Watson, in the words to his classic bluegrass hit "Way Downtown," many have paraphrased the words of 1 Timothy 6:7: "We brought nothing into the world, and we cannot take anything out of the world." Others, such as Rolling Stones guitarist Keith Richards, whose father's remains were placed at the roots of a tree, see only the tree or the gravestone—and nothing beyond. Doc Watson died a confessing Christian, but there are a lot of Keith Richardses out there. As hard as it is to look at, the face of death shakes and breaks our blindness, that the light of Christ's blessed death and resurrection may come. Let us pray for our own constant repentance, and for the repentance of all, throughout this Lententide.

"You are dust, and to dust you shall return" (Genesis 3:19). Although we know the curse of Adam is true, it's far from the whole story. Throughout every moment of repentance and solemn contemplation of Lent, we are forgiven Easter people!

May God the Father, who created this body; may God the Son, who by His blood redeemed this body; may God the Holy Spirit, who by Holy Baptism sanctified this body to be His temple, keep these remains to the day of the resurrection of all flesh. Amen. (*LSB Agenda*, 130)

The Word
of the Lord
Endures Forever

∙∙

I n the name of the Father and of the Son and of the Holy Spirit.
Amen.

Paul's[1] favorite verse:

**I have been crucified with Christ. It is no longer I who live,
but Christ who lives in me. And the life I now live in the
flesh I live by faith in the Son of God, who loved me and
gave Himself for me. I do not nullify the grace of God, for
if righteousness were through the Law, then Christ died
for no purpose.** (Galatians 2:20–21)

Verbum Domini manet in Aeternum. That's on the front of your
service folder. *VDMA.* "The Word of the Lord endures forever." It's a
quote from 1 Peter 1:25, and that was Paul's wondrous motto.

Paul McCain died a long time ago. The Bible, and here St. Paul,
in Paul McCain's favorite verse, speaks in strange ways, and it's so
strange that I think in the Church we get used to it and don't really
understand what Paul is saying by it. "I have been crucified with
Christ." He says my death is Christ's death. It's already been died. He
says I went into death with Christ. When Christ was crucified, I was
crucified. How could this be?

---

1   The Rev. Paul T. McCain (1962–2020) served in numerous capacities within the
Synod, spending the final eighteen years of his life at Concordia Publishing
House as interim president and CEO and as vice president and publisher. He
was one of my dearest friends. His funeral service was December 1, 2020.

Mrs. McCain, you and your husband brought this child, on February 25, 1962, to a font, didn't you? And little Paul was baptized in the name of the Father and of the Son and of the Holy Spirit, just fifty-eight years ago, according to Christ's mandate. Baptism is the Gospel. And you know what's so wonderful about it? It puts Jesus together with us. At that moment, Jesus and Paul were one.

St. Paul says that in Baptism we are clothed with Christ (Galatians 3:27). From that moment on in his life, Paul was a beloved child of God, cleansed in the righteousness of Christ, and seen only as a beloved child. And that lasted until his last breath on this earth. And now it lasts for eternity.

St. Paul said this crucifixion is this: God "made Him to be sin who knew no sin, so that in Him we might become the righteousness of God" (2 Corinthians 5:21). Luther says that when Jesus goes into the water in His Baptism, He puts Himself into the water so that when we go into the water, we bring Jesus out with us. Paul was crucified already fifty-eight years ago. No, already 2,000 years ago.

"It is no longer I who live, but Christ who lives in me." Paul's motto, that of Luther's prince, John Frederick, *verbum Domini manet in aeternum*, the Word of the Lord endures forever, could not be more appropriate for this occasion. Peter says, "You have been born again, not of perishable seed but of imperishable, through the living and abiding Word of God; for 'All flesh is like grass. . . . The grass withers, and the flower falls, but the Word of the Lord remains forever. And this word is the good news that was preached to you" (1 Peter 1:23–25). Baptism, says the apostle, means that all of this is Paul's. And all of it is yours, His perfect life, His perfect love, His suffering, and His resurrection.

So Paul continues to say, and he says it numerous places in the New Testament: "If we have been united with Him in a death like His, we shall certainly be united with Him in a resurrection like His" (Romans 6:5).

Lynn, your husband in this life was a remarkable character. I am honored to have known him so well. He loved you dearly. And I heard him say this many, many times over many, many years. He was amazed at your faith, your strength, your character, and your unbelievable ability. He loved you deeply. Paul and John and Mary, he loved you. He had a special place in his heart for each one of you. I talked to him often about each of you. He hurt when you were in pain or having difficulty. He rejoiced when things were going well for you. And he loved you and prayed for you every single day that you would remain faithful to Christ and His blessed Gospel.

Mrs. McCain, Paul couldn't believe that at your age you went back to school to become a deaconess. And he was delighted by that and proud. And Kirsten, he sent me pictures of the baby and himself last week. And I don't think I have ever seen him so happy. Most of all he cared deeply for all of you and your continued faith in Christ and the reception of Christ's gifts.

In some ways, Paul was a walking contradiction. He would heat up over some issue very quickly, and in half the time he'd be cooled off and have passed it by. I liked to call him a bombastic introvert. He could seem intimidating at first if you didn't know that he was a real big softie inside. I recall him calling me from Dr. Barry's office one time when I was still a pastor in Iowa, and he told me some pretty delicate information about Dr. Barry and some things that were going on. And then he called me the next day and said, "We've got real problems; someone in this office is leaking information, and we can't figure out who it is."

He was a never-ending font of information on the details of Luther, the Lutheran Confessions, Lutheran doctrine, all things theological. And he could present the most deep truths in the most simple, childlike way. And he loved to do that. He loved to preach at St. Paul's Lutheran Church. He loved to teach. He loved to talk to his children about Jesus.

As publisher, with many of you who worked with him, he oversaw what I believe was the greatest decade of Lutheran orthodox publishing in the history of the world outside of Germany. He loved clear Law-and-Gospel preaching, and he often complimented his pastors for it. He detested theological innovation, as distinct from creativity, which dispensed with clear Lutheran categories and distinctions. He loved the clear Scriptures. He loved the Lutheran Confessions. And no one had more intricate and profound understanding of them than he. He made no pretense of this. He loved Luther, Chemnitz, and Gerhard. He retained a lifelong appreciation for seminary professors, particularly Robert Preus for his clear interpretation of the Lutheran Confessions as a living confession and not passe historical documents.

Paul wrote many, many things to which his name was never assigned. He was a very gentle person; he wouldn't hurt a fly. But ironically, his hobby was tactical shooting. This tender introvert could be irascible in theological debate on the internet.

Paul was a damned sinner under the Law, and he knew it. That's why he loved this verse from Galatians [2:12]: "The life I now live in the flesh I live by faith in the Son of God, who loved me and gave Himself for me. I do not nullify the grace of God, for if righteousness were through the law, then Christ died for no purpose."

We are shocked by this death, all of us. I'm still numb. But the Lord is not shocked.

Don't be afraid. You know the Ten Commandments. You know you're sinners. And you know the Gospel. "I do not nullify the grace of God, for if righteousness were through the law, then Christ died for no purpose." "The Word of the Lord endures forever."

Don't be afraid. You know the Creed. Christ "has redeemed me, a lost and condemned person . . . not with gold or silver, but with His holy, precious blood and with His innocent suffering and death" (Small Catechism, Second Article). The Word of the Lord endures forever.

Don't be afraid. You know the Lord's Prayer. You were blessed in this life to have a father and a husband who loved you tenderly. "Our Father who art in heaven. . . . With these words, God tenderly invites us to believe that He is our true Father and that we are His true children, so that with all boldness and confidence we may ask Him as dear children ask their dear father" (Small Catechism, Lord's Prayer, Introduction). He loved me and gave Himself for me. The Word of the Lord endures forever.

Don't be afraid. You know Paul is baptized, and you are too. "Baptism . . . now saves" (1 Peter 3:21). The Word of the Lord endures forever.

Don't be afraid. Paul confessed his sins every week and more in church and received Absolution from the pastor as from God Himself. "If you forgive the sins of any, they are forgiven them" (John 20:23). The Word of the Lord endures forever.

Don't be afraid. Paul received the Sacrament often and with great joy and profound thanks. "Whoever feeds on My flesh and drinks My blood has eternal life, and I will raise him up on the last day" (John 6:54). The Word of the Lord endures forever.

I have been crucified with Christ. It is no longer I who live, but Christ who lives in me. And the life I now live in the flesh I live by faith in the Son of God, who loved me and gave Himself for me. I do not nullify the grace of God, for if righteousness were through the law, then Christ died for no purpose. (Galatians 2:20–21)

The Word of the Lord endures forever. Amen. Come, Lord Jesus.

In the name of the Father and of the Son and of the Holy Spirit. Amen.

Life by Faith in the Son of God

··

The text that Herb[1] chose for this day[2] is from Galatians 2:20:

I have been crucified with Christ. It is no longer I who live, but Christ who lives in me. And the life I now live in the flesh I live by faith in the Son of God, who loved me and gave Himself for me.

Dear friends:

Christ is risen. Alleluia.

All of these texts, you know, were chosen by your dad. And there were many others too. He wanted, as you well know, to make a confession of the faith and also to provide consolation for you. That was his wonderful motive.

If I were you, I would get that funeral plan, with all of its longer sections. I would put it together and print it as a book: *Herb Mueller's Consolations in the Face of Death.* As we were going through the service, there were so many of those lines that I heard him quote over the last year, hymns and verses, from his hospital bed until the time when his voice became labored and he had difficulty getting them out. That is a great blessing.

Illness, suffering, and death are horrid business. This year has been very emotionally and physically draining for you, Faith, and for

---

1   The Rev. Dr. Herbert C. Mueller Jr. (1953–2020) served as a pastor in Illinois for fifteen years before being elected president of the LCMS Southern Illinois District. In 2010 he was elected first vice-president of the LCMS, from which position he retired in 2019.

2   The funeral, held March 25, 2020, was a small, private service.

the whole family. Death and illness, in all its profound effect upon us, is the evidence of the sin that besets us all.

I've struggled over all this, and I'm sure you have too. Your dad had given most of his life in service to Christ and His Church. I didn't want him to retire. But he knew it was time to pay attention to you. He loved you all dearly, very dearly, Nathan, Carey, and Bert, and your spouses and families. I think the only times I saw him weep were the times when he was telling about some pain or challenge you were going through. He loved you dearly, and you know that. It's kind of ironic; he spent so much time in service that you felt his distance from all of you from time to time. He was a workaholic. That's how God built him, I think. Isn't it interesting how God worked to give you Herb this last year? I'm thankful for that.

Herb was a sinner. He knew it, and he'd confess it every day. He knew all of Luther's lines: "I'm a maggot sack." "I'm a poor, miserable this-or-that." And he believed it.

God doesn't act according to our reason. It seemed to me, of anybody who could possibly be said to deserve a long retirement with his wife and family, it was this man. But God doesn't operate according to our mathematics and our logic. And we know that. God is acting according to His cruciform calculations. And Galatians 2:20 lays it out: "I have been crucified with Christ; it is no longer I who live, but Christ. And the life I now live in the flesh, I live by faith in the Son of God who loved me and gave Himself for me."

The New Testament teaches something wondrous. When Paul says, "I have been crucified with Christ," he's talking about Baptism. "We were buried therefore with Him by baptism into death" (Romans 6:4), as we just recited at the beginning of this service. Baptism makes us contemporaneous with Christ. I am baptized with Christ. It clothes us with Christ. Baptism puts us together with Jesus; it puts us in His blessed cruciform arms, with His arms around us. And when the Father sees me, He barely sees me at all. He sees Jesus! He says, "This is My Herb. He's perfect. His sins are forgiven in Me. He is Mine forever." And it's the same thing with you. You are baptized into Christ. The Father sees only Jesus, His perfect one, His perfect Son, fulfilling all the Law, perfectly balancing family and work, making all the perfect decisions, loving, as He should, all the time, forgiving all, covering sins, covering failings, covering evil thoughts, covering challenges and fissures in families. We're all sinners; we all have them.

Jesus says to the Father, "This one has been crucified with Me. This Herb, he no longer lives. But I, Christ, live for him and in him and before You. And the life Herb now lives he lives by Me. I love him. I gave Myself for him. He is Mine. End of story." Or not quite . . .

The crucifixion of Christ was on divine purpose. "The blood of Jesus [God's] Son cleanses us from all sin" (1 John 1:7).

This death of our beloved Herb was on divine purpose. Our lives are "hidden with Christ in God" (Colossians 3:3). We might not know exactly what God is doing; we often don't. But we know the promises. "All things work together for good" (Romans 8:28). "Neither death nor life . . . will be able to separate us from the love of God in Christ Jesus" (Romans 8:38–39).

Although I want to ask God in heaven a few questions about this one, I do know this. This death does what death does for Christians. It gets our attention and places upon our minds things we would not otherwise think about, things that actually matter most, such as being forgiven and reconciled, being a family, loving and treasuring one another as precious gifts, being patient with one another's faults, growing in faith, growing in hope, growing in love right smack in the middle of terrible crosses.

Going to church may be very hard for you for a time. You are going to struggle with emotions, and they're going to come at you at the most unexpected times. There's going to be pain. You will feel joy at times, thankfulness, sorrow. There will be moments when you pull out your phone thinking: "I've got to talk to Dad about this; I've got to share it with him," and all of a sudden, you'll realize you can't do that. There may be depression as reality takes hold. In this struggle, Christ is yours. He's told you, "I've got ahold of you." "If in Christ we have hope in this life only, we are of all people most to be pitied" (1 Corinthians 15:19). The life you live is living by Baptism and faith in the Son of God.

Paul says, "If we have died with Christ, we believe that we will also live with Him" (Romans 6:8). Christ rose from the grave. As Luther says, so much has been done. Christ is the firstfruits to rise again; He's the first one to rise from the grave. And at the last, the trumpet will blow, and Christ Himself will raise us all from the grave.

Christ is risen, and *you* shall see Him on *your* Easter, our great Easter.

You shall see those eyes, the eyes of the Son of God, who said, "I am not a ghost!" You shall see those lips! "Peace be to you!" You shall hear His voice. "A spirit does not have flesh and blood" (Luke 24:39). You shall see His hands. "Come, touch them. See the place where the nails were!" And this very body, these bodies, shall rise in Christ!

And what's more, you shall see your father's eyes again. You shall be kissed by his lips again. This is the radical teaching of the New Testament and its teaching of the resurrection. You shall hear that great, wonderful voice once more, shouting with delight, "You're here! I've been praying for you!" We're told in the Bible that we shouldn't pray to saints, but our Augsburg Confession says we should have no doubt that the saints in heaven are praying for us. Count on it; your dad and your husband is praying for you. And you, Faith, will grab his hand in joy with Christ, for eternity.

"If it were not so," Jesus says, "I would have told you" (John 14:2). And for now: "The life I now live in the flesh I live by faith in the Son of God, who loved me and gave Himself for me."

Christ is risen! Alleluia!

The Courage
of the Martyrs

·····································

What would it take to turn doubting Thomas into fearlessly confessing Thomas? You know Thomas. You know his stubborn rejection of the word from his brothers who had seen the risen Jesus: "Unless I see in His hands the mark of the nails, and place my finger into the mark of the nails, and place my hand into His side, I will never believe" (John 20:25). That sets a pretty high threshold for overcoming doubt.

Jesus didn't have to appear to Thomas. He rose from the dead and appeared to the ten apostles. He didn't need Thomas' faith to accomplish anything. He already rose! It's a done deal. Doubt can't put Jesus back in the grave. And He already delivered His Holy Spirit to the ten apostles and sent them out with His word of absolution on their lips.

Eight days later, again on the first day of the week, Jesus appeared to the apostles. This time Thomas was with them. Instead of starting with a rebuke of Thomas' incredulity and impudence, He simply greeted them with the same peace, and then bid Thomas stick his doubting finger and thrust his unbelieving hand into the still present nail- and spear-wounds of the crucified and risen Lord.

Following Jesus' command, "Do not disbelieve, but believe" (John 20:27), Thomas confessed, "My Lord and my God!" (v. 28). The call of Jesus out of unbelief into faith changed Thomas. We don't know whether he took Jesus up on the invitation to stick his rude finger into the nail holes, nor do we need to know.

From that point, his eyes having seen his crucified and risen Lord, his lips having spoken the beautiful mystery of faith in a God who died and who rose, Thomas was transformed from a coward to a confessor.

Tradition holds that his courageous proclamation of the cross of Christ took Thomas all the way to India. He probably landed on the southwest coast of India around AD 52. There he ministered, proclaimed the Gospel, planted maybe seven churches, baptized numerous families, and ordained pastors to carry on the work. Eventually, he was speared to death for his confession around AD 72 on a mountain in Chennai.

What courage! The sight of the resurrected Jesus completely changed Thomas from a full-fledged skeptic to an intrepid confessor, willing to confess Christ even at the point of the spear. From a doubter to a martyr!

Thomas is hardly alone. All the disciples fled in the garden. Peter denied even knowing Jesus three times! They were all a bunch of cowards! And of the eleven apostles, ten of them were given the blessed death of martyrdom, killed for courageously confessing Christ crucified to the ends of the earth.

Accounts of their martyrdoms are not Scripture. But there's something peculiar about the way the Church has not only preserved and retold these stories but how she has celebrated the stories of martyrdoms. In a world that defines success in terms of longevity, prosperity, and measurable statistics, the church tells stories about her apostles, pastors, and bishops being killed for doing their jobs!

Let the stories of the martyrs encourage you! Paul boasts of his sufferings:

Are they servants of Christ? I am a better one—I am talking like a madman—with far greater labors, far more imprisonments, with countless beatings, and often near death. Five times I received at the hands of the Jews the forty lashes less one. Three times I was beaten with rods. Once I was stoned. Three times I was shipwrecked; a night and a day I was adrift at sea; on frequent journeys, in danger from rivers, danger from robbers, danger from my own people, danger from Gentiles, danger in the city,

danger in the wilderness, danger at sea, danger from false brothers; in toil and hardship, through many a sleepless night, in hunger and thirst, often without food, in cold and exposure. And, apart from other things, there is the daily pressure on me of my anxiety for all the churches. Who is weak, and I am not weak? Who is made to fall, and I am not indignant? If I must boast, I will boast of the things that show my weakness. (2 Corinthians 11:23–30)

Can you imagine a Winkel[1] with the apostle Paul? When most pastors want to boast about their congregation sizes, number of confirmands, and adult Baptisms, Paul wants to talk about who has been beaten with rods more, imprisoned more, or lashed thirty-nine times more!

Get it? Jesus said, "I tell you, My friends, do not fear those who kill the body, and after that have nothing more that they can do" (Luke 12:4). The Lord of the martyrs is the only one in the history of time to defeat death and give His believers a share in that victory over the grave. Courage, friends. He is your Lord too.

---

1 *Winkel* is a German word that means "confidential"; it is the traditional word for the meeting of the pastors in an LCMS circuit.

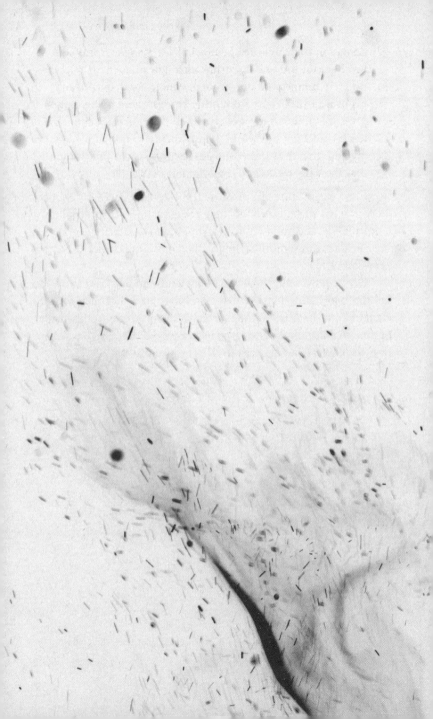

PART IV

Courage
for Shepherds

. . . .

When David faced Goliath, his confidence was in the God who had delivered him from "the paw of the lion and from the paw of the bear" (1 Samuel 17:37). David knew what battle looked like and that he had not protected his sheep with his own power.

Pastors only have one thing going for them when it comes to shepherding their flocks: the holy Word of God. Only one thing, but the only thing worth anything and everything.

Are you a pastor? The Word of the Lord is your strength.

Do you care about your pastor? Bring him the Word as faithfully as he brings it to you.

David's last words are recorded in 2 Samuel 23. Facing death, the shepherd's confidence was unchanged: "For [God] has made with me an everlasting covenant, ordered in all things and secure. For will He not cause to prosper all my help and my desire?" (v. 5).

You know the answer. Yes, yes, it shall be so!

Go to Seminary

S everal factors come into play in the lives of men who end up studying to be pastors. They have a conviction, often growing over time, that being a pastor would be a God-pleasing vocation for which one might be well suited. The Word of God, preached, read, and spoken, works something in the heart and mind of a young man who has come to cherish the Gospel of the free forgiveness of Christ. He begins to consider his own future. His desires are not final or definitive, but they are important. "The saying is trustworthy: If anyone aspires to the office of overseer, he desires a noble task" (1 Timothy 3:1).

St. Paul lists several qualifications for this noble task:

> **Therefore an overseer must be above reproach, the husband of one wife, sober-minded, self-controlled, respectable, hospitable, able to teach, not a drunkard, not violent but gentle, not quarrelsome, not a lover of money. He must manage his own household well, with all dignity keeping his children submissive, for if someone does not know how to manage his own household, how will he care for God's church? He must not be a recent convert, or he may become puffed up with conceit and fall into the condemnation of the devil. Moreover, he must be well thought of by outsiders, so that he may not fall into disgrace, into a snare of the devil.** (1 Timothy 3:2–7)

Can a young man, preparing to head to the seminary, live up to these biblical requirements to be a pastor? Well, not really. He is embarking on a journey to grow into the office that he will occupy, and hopefully, he will never stop growing in Christ. It takes an intricate synthesis of intrepidity and spiritual caution. The apostolic mandates tell us a pastor will have to be a man of genuine faith in Christ and have a life that reflects that, along with a good reputation and ability to teach. Our seminary entrance process evaluates a man, including his potential to serve in the capacity of pastor, weaknesses and all.

By the end of his rigorous study, the student's doctrine and life are well known. The seminaries together with the Council of Presidents present qualified men to be called by congregations of the Synod. That call is a formal, divine call accomplished by the actions of God Himself through a congregation or congregations in fellowship and cooperation with the broader church. After examination of doctrine and life and a call by a congregation or Synod (for example, as a missionary), a man is ordained and placed into the office. In the ordination, the whole church acknowledges that this man is a pastor. "No one should publicly teach in the Church, or administer the Sacraments, without a rightly ordered call," that is, without examination, call, and ordination (Augsburg Confession XIV).

Young man, go to one of our seminaries—Fort Wayne or St. Louis. You will not regret it. You will learn. You will study the Bible in the original languages. You will delight in Christ and in a richness in His Scriptures that will dramatically alter your life. You might enter the seminary convinced by your friends and family that you are quite amazing, with an incomparable personality. But trust me, you are entering on a journey that will humble you and bring you to realize you are nothing and that Christ is everything. You will learn to gift your people with Christ. You will learn that your personality cannot carry the day and go the distance against sin, death, and the devil. You will come to nothing, that Christ may be all in all.

The greatest adventure of your life will be sharing Jesus with those who do not know Him—with the tired, the beaten, the sinner, the mentally ill, the suffering. It will be all the more meaningful for you as you suffer crosses yourself. And at the last you shall say, "So you also, when you have done all that you were commanded, say, 'We are unworthy servants; we have only done what was our duty'" (Luke 17:10). "Well done, good and faithful servant" (Matthew 25:21).

Pray to the Lord of the Harvest

....

I pray the catechism every day like my little Hans and ask God to keep me in his dear, holy Word, lest I grow weary of it.[1]

For the longest time, I wondered what Luther meant by that. Then Concordia Publishing House invited me to provide a fresh translation of Martin Luther's *A Simple Way to Pray*, written for Peter, Master Barber. Luther was sitting in the barber's chair one day in 1535 when his barber asked him how to pray. He responded with a delightful little pamphlet on the topic. There Luther described a method, no doubt developed during his years as an Augustinian friar. It's a method that can be used with any text of the Bible, the catechism, or even a hymn. It has four parts: (1) Instruction; (2) Thanksgiving; (3) Confession; (4) Prayer (I.T.C.P.).

I recommend reading Luther's pamphlet. He encourages allowing one's mind to wander as the Spirit prompts thoughts and prayers based on the text. Should we pray written prayers or prayers *ex corde* ("from the heart")? Luther answered, "Yes!"

In the next fifteen years, half of the current LCMS pastors will retire. Seminary numbers are now very low. And there is a strong need for LCMS-trained schoolteachers and administrators now! With these kinds of needs for "laborers in the harvest," allow me to demonstrate Luther's method of prayer, based on the words of Jesus.

---

1   *Table Talk* no. 1727, AE 54:163.

When He saw the crowds, He had compassion for them, because they were harassed and helpless, like sheep without a shepherd. Then He said to His disciples, "The harvest is plentiful, but the laborers are few; therefore pray earnestly to the Lord of the harvest to send out laborers into His harvest." (Matthew 9:36–38)

1. *Instruction.* Dear Jesus, in Your earthly ministry in Palestine, You demonstrated the utmost compassion for the "harassed and helpless." You grieved over people who were "like sheep without a shepherd." You teach us in Your Word that the fields shall be ripe for harvest until Your return, and that Your Church needs workers to have compassion and proclaim the Gospel. You also instruct us that when workers are needed, the place to begin is with prayer.

2. *Thanksgiving.* O Christ, I thank You for my pastor. I thank You for the pastor who baptized me. I thank You for my confirmation pastor. I thank You for the seminaries. I thank You for all faithful pastors. I thank You for our dear Lutheran teachers. I thank You for our Concordias. I thank You for all the thousands of young women and men who are entering the sacred calling of teacher. I thank You for the thousands of selfless church workers who have chosen lives of modest means for the sake of serving Your sheep.

3. *Confession.* I confess, O Lord, that I have failed to recognize what a great blessing my pastors have been. I have thought little of the thousands upon thousands who teach our children and youth in the schools of the LCMS. I have been stingy in my support of my own congregation and have barely given a thought to supporting the church's seminaries and universities. I have failed to express my thanks and love to our congregations' pastors and teachers. I have failed to pray for them. I have even sinned by thinking ill of them or gossiping about them. And I have ignored Your very own words directed to me, "Pray the Lord of the harvest to send out laborers." I think

little of the very reason Your Church exists: "The harvest is plentiful." I deserve to have Your precious pastors and teachers taken from me.

4. *Prayer.* O merciful Savior! Look not upon my manifold and horrid sins! I plead Your precious sacrifice on the cross for me! I plead Your resurrection, absolving the world and me from sin! I plead my Baptism! Lord, forgive me! Lord, strengthen my love for Your Word and for Your faithful pastors and teachers! Cause me to be a joy to them in all I do! Help me to pray daily for them! Remind me that the gifts these workers bring me are to be shared with the harassed and helpless! Make me generous in my support for them! Lord, make me cognizant of Your words every day of my life: "The harvest is plentiful, but the laborers are few; therefore pray earnestly to the Lord of the harvest to send out laborers into His harvest."

The Lord's Prayer, the Our Father, is the great standard for all of our prayers. When God invites us to approach Him as our Father, He teaches us to bring our requests to Him "with all boldness and confidence" (Small Catechism, Lord's Prayer, Introduction). The God of heaven and earth has promised to hear us! Ask, dear child, for laborers for the harvest, and see what will be given to you.

How Shall They Hear without a Preacher?

. . . .

So faith comes from hearing, and hearing through the word of Christ" (Romans 10:17). Over and again, Luther emphasized the orality of the New Testament message. The Word of God is to be preached. St. Paul explains in Romans 10:

> For with the heart man believeth unto righteousness; and with the mouth confession is made unto salvation. . . . For whosoever shall call upon the name of the Lord shall be saved. How then shall they call on Him in whom they have not believed? and how shall they believe in Him of whom they have not heard? and how shall they hear without a preacher? And how shall they preach, except they be sent? as it is written, How beautiful are the feet of them that preach the gospel of peace, and bring glad tidings of good things! . . . So then faith cometh by hearing, and hearing by the word of God. (Romans 10:10–17 KJV)

Paul says that faith grabs hold of Jesus and confesses aloud who Jesus is for salvation. All who call upon the name of the Lord shall be saved. But that can't happen where Jesus is not believed. Belief can't happen where the message has not been heard. There can be no hearing of the message without a preacher. And there's no preacher if one is not sent. How beautiful are the preacher's feet. Those feet go! Feet going, mouth preaching the Gospel of peace and glad tidings— that's the pastoral office in a nutshell.

But can't the Gospel be proclaimed by the layperson? Certainly! Remember the Samaritan woman whom Jesus met at the well, and how many of the Samaritans of that city believed in Jesus because of the woman's witness (John 4:39)? Don't we all have the responsibility of proclaiming Christ? Certainly. We speak Christ and His forgiveness in our families, to our friends—in short, wherever the Lord has put us to be His disciples. We also have the responsibility of making sure the Word of Christ is proclaimed *officially* among us, in our congregations and through planting new churches. We see Paul, for instance, making provision in his epistles for more called and ordained workers who hold the *office* of pastor. He was following Jesus' mandate: "The harvest is plentiful, but the laborers are few. Therefore pray earnestly to the Lord of the harvest to send out laborers into His harvest" (Luke 10:2).

Over the next fifteen years, one-half of the current active clergy of the LCMS will reach retirement age. Seminary class numbers have been small in recent years. Even with an increase of multipoint parishes in both rural and urban settings, we will still need more pastors.

What can you do? First, pray to the Lord of the harvest to send workers. The Lord commands us so to pray and shall hear our prayers. Second, treat your pastor like the gift he is—a man with "Good News" feet and a Gospel mouth. A faithful pastor works hard, preaching, visiting, praying, and delivering the Sacraments. He needs all the love and support he can get. Third, encourage young men to visit our seminaries and to consider a life dedicated to preaching Christ's Gospel, caring for Christ's holy people, and seeking those who shall yet come to faith in Christ. "Faith comes from hearing, and hearing through the word of Christ" (Romans 10:17).

Law and Gospel in Times of Trial

....

In trying to find parallels to the COVID-19 epidemic, mention is often made of the Spanish flu outbreak in 1918. But there have been other epidemics in the United States that were far more dangerous than the flu in 1918 or COVID-19, serious as they were. In St. Louis, cholera struck in 1849. Of St. Louis' 63,471 residents, 8,444 died. At its worst, two hundred people a day were dying in the city.

Dr. C. F. W. Walther's family was hit by the deaths of his mother-in-law, sister-in-law, and nephew, all in June. That year he performed funerals for forty-five members of his congregation struck down by the disease. Another local LCMS pastor noted after a visit to St. Louis in 1849 that he saw "hearses from morning till night, without ceasing." On top of all this, there was a terrible Ascension Day fire that May that destroyed six hundred buildings and twenty-seven steamships moored on the banks of the Mississippi. Many of the members of Trinity Lutheran Church were also suffering from that devastation of homes and businesses. Dr. Walther himself was named the health official of his district, responsible "to use such remedies as necessity demands by supplying the poor with medical devices, having medicines made up for them, and using disinfectants."

What did Dr. Walther preach during these hard times?

Rebellions by entire nations against their governments;[1] bloody, destructive wars on land and sea; a contagious epidemic striding across the face of the earth; these are

---

1   1848 saw numerous revolutions against European governments.

the awesome preachers to whom God has now issued the command: "Go into all the world and preach repentance to all creatures!"[2]

That was a clever turn. Walther applied Christ's mandate to preach repentance to the devastating events happening in the world of his hearers in 1849! But times of fear, death, and destruction often amount to the preaching of Law. They terrify and strike down, revealing sin, faithlessness, and fear.

What should a preacher preach? Indeed, to the suffering, the discouraged, the downtrodden, those struck by tragedy, the preacher proclaims the pure sweet Gospel of Christ. "Come to Me, all who labor and are heavy laden, and I will give you rest" (Matthew 11:28). "I am the resurrection and the life. Whoever believes in Me, though he die, yet shall he live" (John 11:25). "For God so loved the world, that He gave His only Son, that whoever believes in Him should not perish but have eternal life" (John 3:16).

Crises strike us in different ways, producing different results and different sins. Some doubt God's promises. Some become paralyzed by fear. Some take on an epicurean attitude: "Let's eat and drink, for tomorrow we die!" Some become selfish and self-centered. Some become overbearing, disdaining others with a different view. Some "despise preaching and His Word" or the Lord's Supper.

For the moment, it seemed that many people had little to fear from COVID-19 itself. But some were struck hard, suffered for weeks or longer, and even died. Some areas of the country were walloped; others, not so much. The uncertainty of the situation caused division within congregations, and the legal and social steps taken in the name of safety created another category of difficulties. One pastor commented, "I thought I had a 'purple' congregation, but I discovered during COVID that I had two congregations: one blue and one red."

This all shows preaching and pastoral care to be a thorny calling. Pastoral care is the art of distinguishing the Law and the Gospel and

---

2 C. F. W. Walther, *The Word of His Grace* (Lake Mills, IA: Graphic Publishing, 1978), 167.

giving each its due. Luther called properly distinguishing between Law and Gospel the most difficult task of being a pastor.

I suggest two things: First, cut your pastor some slack. He's not Jesus. He's regularly dealing with tough situations in which people have diverse and strong opinions. Second, despite the views you've formulated on what your pastor or congregation has done or should do, put your hand to your chest, and feel whether you have flesh and blood, and at least believe what the Scriptures say: "None is righteous, no, not one" (Romans 3:10). When you have reason to, go to your pastor and say, "Pastor, I'm sorry I've been a pain to you and made your life challenging. Please forgive me. I want to do better. How can I be helpful?" And he shall say, "I do forgive you. In the stead of Christ, and by His command, I forgive you all your sins in the name of the Father and of the Son and of the Holy Spirit. Amen."

Are You Okay, Pastor?

. . . .

We can probably agree that we have been through very tumultuous and troubling days. I also think you'll agree that the troubling political, economic, and racial tensions in our society are reflected in the church, like it or not. We were all drained by the uncertainty and unknowns forced on us by COVID. An extensive survey from the Secretary of Synod's office, which included data from some 2,000 congregations, asked how the virus had affected our congregations and people through June 2020. Although some expressed weariness and anxiety, especially among our smaller congregations, most were doing okay. Some 25 percent had experienced increased giving, for instance. Our congregations with schools were very concerned. We now know that in many places grade school enrollments actually increased because of uncertainty in public schools over the virus.

But the weariness lingers. As I'm in contact with pastors, congregations, and district leaders, I note that pastors are worn down. They were called upon for additional church services, online services, and dealing with the different viewpoints of members, all within a shifting sea of local regulations. For long months there was only gnawing uncertainty. Would young families come back to church? When could we restart Sunday school, if at all? Had dear families opted not to attend church, or were they seeking what they wanted elsewhere? Was reception of the forgiveness of sins through the Word and the blessed Sacraments the main thing to our people? Would they live and die in the faith? Giving has slowed; what does this mean?

Perhaps the most sorrowful lament I hear from pastors is that, because of pandemic restrictions, they were not allowed to minister to the dying. These were not only congregants, but they were the dearest of beloved brothers and sisters in Christ, dear friends! This is the very thing a pastor is given to do for his people. What pangs of conscience, what sorrow is suffered, when this kind of critical pastoral care cannot be carried out!

It all wears on a pastor's heart. He knows full well the verse spoken at his installation and ordination: "Pay careful attention to yourselves and to all the flock, in which the Holy Spirit has made you overseers, to care for the church of God, which He obtained with His own blood" (Acts 20:28).

As president of the Synod, I have not the slightest ability or mandate to tell you what to do, much less to make you do it. I wouldn't want it any other way. But I implore you, by the mercy of Jesus Christ, to love your pastor. Christ has blessed you with the clear knowledge of the free Gospel of forgiveness in the cross and resurrection. He has given you a congregation of fellow believers. He has given you a pastor, perhaps a lifetime of pastors, to love you in Christ and to care for you. Please care for your pastor. He's called by God through your congregation to call you to repent of your sins daily and to proclaim that Christ's forgiveness is yours.

Now is the time, like no other, to be generous to your congregation by going to your pastor and telling him you are glad to have him. Stand ready and willing to hold up the prophet's arms (Exodus 17:12). Tell him, "I'm praying for you, Pastor." Thank him for things he's done wisely and for times when his initiative has helped those in need or put out fires. Speak well of him to other members of your congregation and community. Ask him, "Is your family okay, Pastor? Are you doin' okay?" Elders, tell your pastor, "The Bible tells us that we are to care for each other, Pastor. That means we're here to care for you!"

Epilogue

. . . .

Lately, one of my favorite sections of the Book of Concord has been this excerpt from the Solid Declaration of the Formula of Concord. It speaks volumes to how we navigate life surrounded by perils aplenty. It has greatly encouraged me. I pray it does the same for you too.

> **Furthermore, this doctrine [of election] provides glorious consolation under the cross and amid temptations. In other words, God in His counsel, before the time of the world, determined and decreed that He would assist us in all distresses. He determined to grant patience, give consolation, nourish and encourage hope, and produce an outcome for us that would contribute to our salvation. Also, Paul teaches this in a very consoling way. He explains that God in His purpose has ordained before the time of the world by what crosses and sufferings He would conform every one of His elect to the image of His Son. His cross shall and must work together for good for everyone, because they are called according to God's purpose. Therefore, Paul has concluded that it is certain and beyond doubt that neither "tribulation, or distress," neither "death nor life," or other such things "will be able to separate us from the love of God in Christ Jesus our Lord."** (Solid Declaration of the Formula of Concord XI 48–49)

Every cross has a purpose. Every trial is ordained by God from the foundation of the world to shape us into the image of His Son. On top of that, in all distresses, God has "determined and decreed that He would assist us." He will "grant patience, give consolation, nourish and encourage hope, and produce an outcome for us that would contribute to our salvation."

Jesus Himself gives courage. *Take courage*, He says; *your sins are forgiven*. With forgiveness in our hearts and on our lips, nothing daunts our courage.

Take courage, Jesus says; *I have overcome the world*. If He has overcome the world, our sin, and the power of the devil, we have nothing left to fear.

Take courage, Jesus says; *it is I.*